Bulbous plants of Turkey and Iran

(including the adjacent Greek Islands)

A photographic guide
by *Peter Sheasby*

Charity No. 207478
Alpine Garden Society, AGS Centre, Avon Bank, Pershore WR10 3JP, UK

© Alpine Garden Society 2007

First published 2007

All rights reserved. No part of this book may be translated, reproduced or transmitted in any form or by any means (electronic or mechanical, including photocopying, recording or by any information storage and retrieval system) except brief extracts by a reviewer for the purpose of review, without written permission of the copyright owners

ISBN 978 0 90 004877 7

Design and origination by Blenheim Colour Ltd. www.blencolour.com
Diagrams and maps by Richard Morris
Printed by Information Press Ltd, Eynsham, Oxford

Contents

Introduction 4
   Maps 6
   Glossary 8
   Habitat Descriptions 9
   Habitat Photographs 10

Ranunculaceae 17
   Anemone 18
   Eranthis 18
   Ranunculus 18

Berberidaceae 25
   Bongardia 25
   Leontice 25

Fumariaceae 27
   Corydalis 27

Primulaceae 35
   Cyclamen 35

Araceae 43
   Arum 44
   Biarum 48
   Eminium 51
   Arisarum 52
   Dracunculus 52

Asphodelaceae 53
   Asphodelus 53
   Eremurus 55
   Asphodeline 58
   Anthericum 60

Alliaceae 61
   Allium 61
   Nectaroscordum 72

Hyacinthaceae 73
   Urginea 74
   Dipcadi 74
   Scilla 75
   Chionodoxa 81
   Puschkinia 83
   Ornithogalum 85
   Muscari 94
   Hyacinthus 104
   Bellevalia 106
   Hyacinthella 111
   Alrawia 111

Liliaceae 113
   Lilium 114
   Fritillaria 119

Tulipa	138	Epipactis	236
Erythronium	150	Neottia	240
Gagea	151	Limodorum	240

Colchicaceae   159

Merendera	160	Epipogium	240
Colchicum	163	Goodyera	240

Amaryllidaceae   173

Sternbergia	174	Spiranthes	240
Leucojum	176	Plantanthera	240
Galanthus	177	Ophrys	243
Ixiolirion	181	Serapias	255
Narcissus	181	Aceras	257
Pancratium	181	Himantoglossum	257
Ungernia	181	Barlia	257

Iridaceae   185

Iris	186	Neotinea	257
Hermodactylus	207	Traunsteinera	257
Gynandriris	207	Steveniella	257
Crocus	208	Comperia	257
Romulea	228	Orchis	260
Gladiolus	230	Dactylorhiza	269

Orchidaceae   235

Index   274

Cephalanthera	236	Bibliography	279
		Photographic Credits	280

Introduction

This photographic guide is intended to help in the identification of bulbous plants that are found in the wild in Turkey and Iran and in the Greek islands on the western fringes of Turkey. It gives limited descriptions of the species, particularly when they are easily recognisable from the photographs, and is best used in conjunction with other books providing greater botanical detail. However, with more difficult groups it attempts to give guidance on characteristics that help to narrow down the choice of species to be considered.

The term 'bulbous' is used in its widest sense, so the book covers plants with bulbous, cormous, tuberous and rhizomatous roots, as might be found in a typical 'bulb' catalogue. The bulk of the species are monocotyledons in the *Araceae*, *Asphodelaceae*, *Alliaceae*, *Hyacinthaceae*, *Liliaceae*, *Colchicaceae*, *Amaryllidaceae*, *Iridaceae* and *Orchidaceae* families, but some dicotyledons such as *Anemone*, *Corydalis* and *Cyclamen* species are also included. The families appear in their generally accepted order. The main botanical and nomenclatural sources have been Flora of Turkey (P. H. Davis), including the recent revisions of Volume 11, and Flora Iranica (K. H. Rechinger). More recently named species have been added where possible, and modern reviews of genera such as *Cyclamen*, *Crocus*, *Galanthus* and *Tulipa* have been consulted. The recent division of *Liliaceae* has been incorporated but no attempt has been made to adopt the present changes in *Orchis*.

Plants are classified on the basis of their flower and fruit structure and some knowledge of these is needed (see Diags. 1 and 2), but in general, botanical terms have been kept to a minimum, where special terms are needed, they have been explained in the glossary.

The book starts with general views of the terrain in botanically interesting areas of Turkey and Iran, and then describes a range of the individual species present.

The species photographs appear after each group of species descriptions, and the locality in which the plant has been photographed is indicated. Not all species have been photographed in Turkey, the adjacent Greek Islands or Iran, and some have been illustrated in cultivation rather than in the wild, but wherever possible the photographs are of species in the wild in the areas concerned. The distribution of the species (**Dist:**) is shown below each photograph, and a bar chart indicates the months in which it is usually in flower.

The terms used in the description of plant distributions in Turkey need some explanation, as the name 'Turkey' is only used in connection with the part of Turkey in Europe (Turkey-in-Europe) and the NW and western fringes of Turkey. For other parts of Turkey (i.e. the majority) the term 'Anatolia' is used. The way in which the different parts of Anatolia are designated is indicated on the map, and this generally follows those used in The Flora of Turkey (P. H. Davis). Also following this convention, the Greek East Aegean Islands close to the Turkish coast, such as Lesbos, Samos, Chios and Rhodes, are included in the area covered. Some mention of Cyprus is also made. In the case of Iran, distribution is indicated in very broad terms such as N Iran or W Iran, but very important areas are the Alborz (Elburz) Mountains in the north and the Zagros Mountains in the west.

Both countries have a large and diverse flora, and this arises from the many influences coming from different geographical directions. Western Turkey and the adjacent Greek Islands have the extensive flora typical of the eastern Mediterranean, and this is modified in S Anatolia by the Middle Eastern influences coming from Syria and Iraq. In the SE there are similarities with the flora of NW Iran, and in the NE the high plateaus and wetter mountains have species in common with the Caucasus area. The mountains facing the Black Sea coast are again different with their very high rainfall and temperate rain forest. In the centre the Anatolian plain is generally much drier and hotter. Another influence is the so-called 'Anatolian Diagonal', which is a line of mountains running from the eastern Taurus in the south to the Pontic Alps in the NE. This has provided a significant barrier to the East-West movement of plant species.

In Iran the Caspian Sea has a similar influence to the Black Sea, and the northern Alborz Mountains are relatively wet, and support extensive forests. The NW has many similarities to SE Turkey, and this influence is carried into the Zagros Mountains in the west. The NE is much drier, but areas such as Golestan still support extensive deciduous woodlands at the lower levels. The eastern and southern regions are much drier, and much of the centre is semi-desert.

In both countries some plants are only found very locally, and some are under threat from development, agricultural changes and other human influences such as the digging of bulbs from the wild. Readers should therefore be reminded that it is illegal to collect plant material from either country without official permission.

Acknowledgements
Many people have helped in the preparation of this book, especially in the provision of photographs, but the author would particularly like to acknowledge the help of Alan Edwards, Rene Gämperle, Ian Green, Eric Pasche and Bob and Rannveig Wallis. Useful discussions have taken place with Ian Green, Brian Mathew, John Page, Professor John Richards and David Stephens, and Ann Thomas has helped with proof reading. The support of the Alpine Garden Society has been crucial in their agreement to publish the book, and thanks go to Professor John Good, Director of Publications and Christine McGregor, the Society Director. Finally the staff of Blenheim Colour Ltd. have contributed a great deal in the design and setting of the book and the scanning of the photographic images.

Maps

Map of Turkey and the adjacent Greek Islands

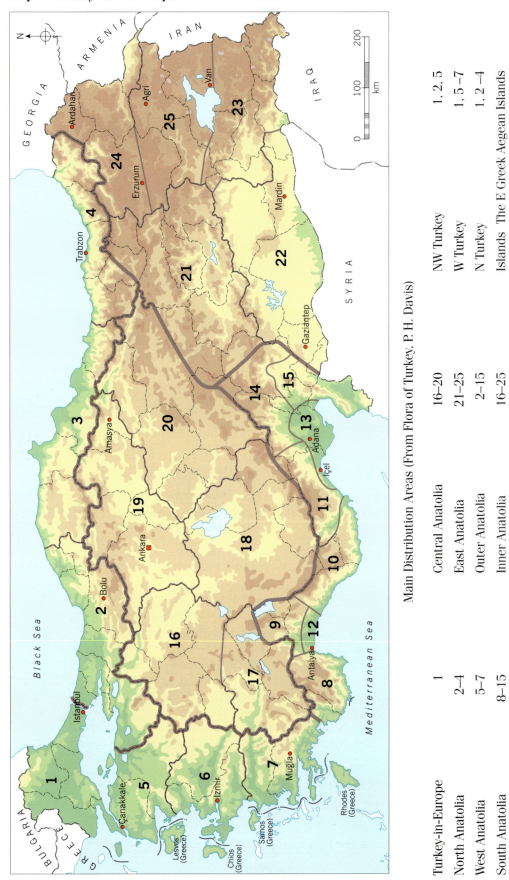

Maps

Map of Iran

Golestan, NE Iran

Glossary

Glossary *(from Mediterranean Wild Flowers, M. Blamey and C. Grey-Wilson, 1993)*

Anther	The upper part of the stamen that carries the pollen.	Membranous	Thin and dry, often opaque or transparent.
Auricle	Small ear-like projections (see *Cyclamen*).	Nectary	A nectar-producing organ, often located at the base of a petal (see *Fritillaria*).
Axil	The angle between the leaf and the stem.	Ovary	The female organ containing one or more ovules, which after fertilisation develops into the fruit.
Bract	A small scale-like or leaf-like organ located where the flower stalk (the pedicel) meets the stem.	Pedicel	The stalk of an individual flower.
Bulb	An underground storage organ developed from the fleshy base of leaves or scales, with or without an outer skin or tunic (e.g. *Lilium*).	Perianth	A collective word for all the floral parts, petals and sepals.
		Petiole	The leaf stalk.
Calyx	The collective name for the sepals of a flower.	Raceme	A spike-like inflorescence in which the individual flowers are stalked.
Cataphyll	A membranous sheath that encloses the leaves and/or inflorescence as they come up through the ground (e.g. in *Colchicum*).	Rhizome	An underground or surface stem, often thick and swollen (e.g. *Iris*).
		Sessile	Without a stalk.
Ciliate	Fringed with hairs.	Scape	A leafless stem bearing flowers.
Claw	A narrow lower part of a petal or sepal (see *Iris*).	Spadix	The central spike of an *Araceae* inflorescence that carries the flowers at the base.
Corm	A swollen underground organ produced from the swollen stem base; generally annual with a new corm arising on top of the old one (e.g. *Crocus*).	Spathe	A large bract-like organ that envelops or partly envelops the inflorescence (see *Araceae*).
Corolla	The collective name for the petals of a flower.	Spur	A hollow, cylindrical structure projecting from the corolla and generally containing nectar (see *Orchis*).
Corona	A cup-shaped projection from the centre of a flower (see *Puschkinia*).	Standard	The inner perianth segments of the *Iris* flower.
Corymb	A compound inflorescence with the lower branches longer than the upper so that all end up at the same level.	Stigma	The receptive tip of the style to which pollen grains adhere.
Endemic	Confined to one region.	Style	The stalk that connects the stigma to the ovary.
Entire	Margins of leaves or petals that are without teeth.	Subspecies	A subdivision of a species differentiated by several characters, and also geographically or ecologically.
Falcate	Sickle-shaped, for example of leaves.	Tepal	The inner and outer perianth segments of plants such as *Tulipa* where both are essentially the same (see *Liliaceae*).
Falls	The outer perianth segments of an Iris flower.		
Filament	The stalk of a stamen.	Tessellated	Chequered (see *Colchicum* and *Fritillaria*).
Glabrous	Without hairs.		
Glaucous	Covered with a waxy bloom, giving a bluish or greyish colouration.	Tuber	A swollen underground organ, developed from underground stems, or sometimes from the roots (e.g. *Orchidaceae*).
Inflorescence	The flowering branch or branches.		
Lamina	The blade of a petal or leaf (see *Iris*).	Umbel	An inflorescence in which all the branches arise from the same point, like the spokes of an umbrella.
Lax	Loose.		
Linear	Narrow and parallel-sided.	Variety	A subdivision of a species or subspecies, often differing in a single character, and often growing with or close to the typical plant.
Lip	A petal or petals which form a distinct part of the flower and act as a landing place for visiting insects (see *Orchidaceae*).		
		Whorl	More than two organs arising from the same point on a stem (leaves or flowers).

Flower Structure/Habitat Descriptions

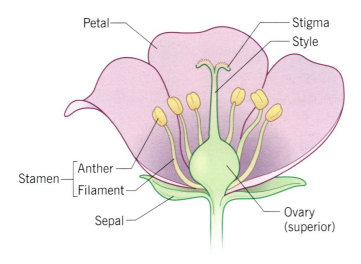

Diagram 1: Typical flower structure (superior ovary)

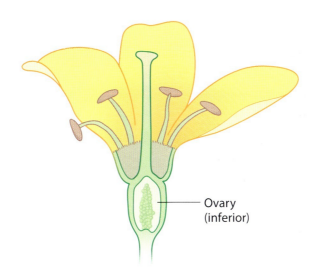

Diagram 2: Flower with inferior ovary

Habitat Descriptions

Macchie	A dense community of evergreen shrubs and small trees, usually 1-3m in height.	Steppe	Dry, open grassland, often dominated by plants that are resistant to grazing.
Phrygana	A more open community of dwarf evergreen shrubs, which allows smaller plant and bulb species to flourish. Grazing maintains this habitat.	Oak Scrub	This is a type of phrygana where the dominant tree is a *Quercus* species such as *Q. coccifera, Q. petraea, Q. libani* or *Q. infectoria*.

Habitat Photographs

Dam on the River Euphrates, S Anatolia

Ak Dağ in the Taurus Mountains in autumn

Eranthis hyemalis on Gembos Yayla, Nr. Ibradi, S Anatolia

Habitat Photographs

Lake Eğridir, S Anatolia

Zigana Pass, Trabzon, NE Anatolia

Çam Pass, Ardahan, NE Anatolia

Habitat Photographs

Iris caucasica on Çam Pass, NE Anatolia

Çoruh Valley, NE Anatolia

Colchicum speciosum on Ilgaz Dağ, N Anatolia

Habitat Photographs

Nemrut Dağ Crater, Lake Van, SE Anatolia

Muradiye River, E Anatolia

Karabet Pass, SE Anatolia

Habitat Photographs

Tea Plantations, Rize, NE Anatolia

Caspian Woodlands, N Iran

Hills near Shulabad, W Iran

Karun Valley, W Iran

Habitat Photographs

Zagros Mountains
near Chelgerd, W Iran

Fritillaria imperialis
near Chelgerd, W Iran

Southern Alborz
Mountains, N Iran

Habitat Photographs

Aghdak Valley, W Iran

Golestan Reserve, N Iran

Olang Mountain, N Iran

Ranunculaceae

The buttercup family is not generally 'bulbous', but several genera in the family have cormous, tuberous or bulbous roots, notably *Anemone, Eranthis* and *Ranunculus* itself. Illustrations of the relevant species of *Anemone* and *Eranthis* present in Turkey and Iran are included, but, in the case of *Ranunculus*, only a few selected species are shown.

Ranunculaceae: *Anemone/Eranthis/Ranunculus*

Anemone

Anemone coronaria (Figs. 1, 2) and ***A. pavonina* (Fig. 3)** are nominally similar species, but the three bracts below the flowers, in the case of *A. coronaria* are divided more than once, and with *A. pavonina* they are simple or mainly so. Both occur in red, violet, pink and white forms. They are mainly distributed near the Mediterranean coasts of Turkey and on some of the Islands. *Anemone coronaria* is also found in W Iran.

Anemone blanda (Figs. 4, 5) and ***A. caucasica* (Fig.6)** are closely related, but *A. caucasica* has smaller flowers and is only found in NE Anatolia. *A. blanda* is widely distributed and is usually found in open woodland situations, but it also grows in stony places high in the mountains, often near melting snow. Both species occur in blue and white forms. *Anemone caucasia* is also found in N Iran.

Anemone biflora also occurs in two colour forms, yellow and red **(Figs. 7, 8)**, both of which are found in Iran.

Anemone petiolulosa (Fig. 9) is an eastern species which reaches the N and E of Iran in the Khorasan area. It grows in stony places in the mountains, and is similar to *A. biflora* but the flowers are smaller and more open, and the leaves are more divided.

Anemone tschernjaewi (Fig. 10) is mainly found to the east of our area, but it has been rarely reported from NE Iran.

The widely distributed *Anemone nemorosa* is also present in the Istanbul area, and non-tuberous species *A. narcissiflora* and *A. albana* are found in the mountains.

Eranthis

Only one species, **Eranthis hyemalis (Fig. 11)** is found in Turkey. This is the form with larger flowers and narrower leaf segments sometimes separated as *E. cilicicus*. Another species is found in Iran, and this is **Eranthis longistipitata (Fig. 12)** which grows in scrub near Mashhad in the NE Corner of Iran. It has smaller flowers than *E. hyemalis* and seed pods that are on long stalks rather than being sessile.

Ranunculus

Ranunculus asiaticus (Fig. 13) is a very large-flowered buttercup, which in many ways resembles the larger *Anemone* species but it has sepals. It also occurs in many colours including red, yellow and white, but in Turkey only the red form is found. It grows in S Anatolia and the Islands, and in W Iran.

Several forms of our lesser celandine, *Ranunculus ficaria*, occur and a large-flowered, large-leaved form, **Ranunculus ficaria ssp. calthifolia** is illustrated **(Fig. 14)**. The closely related **R. kochii (Fig. 15)** is found high in the mountains of E Anatolia and W and N Iran, usually close to melting snow.

The next three species are all small, low-growing species with tuberous roots, and they are found in high mountain areas. **Ranunculus myosuroides (Fig. 16)** grows in damp, bare soil near melting snow in the Anti-Taurus and Kurdistan areas of Anatolia. Its name comes from the fact that the fruiting centre of the flower elongates rapidly to be twice as long as the stamens, making it resemble a small *Myosurus*.

The form of **Ranunculus cadmicus** illustrated is **ssp. cyprius** from Cyprus **(Fig. 17)**, but the Turkish forms are very similar. It grows on mountain slopes at about 2,000m in W and S Anatolia.

The final species, **Ranunculus unguis-cati (Fig. 18)**, is very localised and is only found in the Maraş area of S Anatolia. It grows in stony ground at high levels on Ahir Dağ near Kahramanmaraş.

Ranunculaceae: *Anemone*

Anemone coronaria
Nr. Manavgat, S Anatolia
Dist: Outer Anatolia and Islands, W Iran
J **F M A** M J J A S O N D

Anemone coronaria
Island of Chios
Dist: Outer Anatolia and Islands, W Iran
J **F M A** M J J A S O N D

Anemone pavonina
Island of Chios
Dist: NW Turkey, Islands
J F **M A** M J J A S O N D

Ranunculaceae: *Anemone*

Anemone blanda
Nr. Antalya, S Anatolia
Dist: Scattered throughout Anatolia except SE
J **F M A** M J J A S O N D

Anemone blanda
Mountain form on Ahir Dağ, S Anatolia,
Dist: Scattered throughout Anatolia except SE
J **F M A** M J J A S O N D

Anemone caucasica
Zagar Pass, Georgia
Dist: NE Anatolia and N Iran
J F M **A M** J J A S O N D

Ranunculaceae: *Anemone*

Anemone biflora
Golestan, N Iran
Dist: N and W Iran
J F **M A** M J J A S O N D

Fig 007

Anemone biflora
Nr. Semirom, W Iran
Dist: N and W Iran
J F **M A** M J J A S O N D

Fig 008

Anemone petiolulosa
Dzhabagly, Kazakhstan
Dist: N and E Iran
J F **M A** M J J A S O N D

Fig 009

Ranunculaceae: *Anemone/Eranthis*

Anemone tschernjaewi
Nr. Khomeyn, N Iran
Dist: **N Iran**
J F **M A M** J J A S O N D

Eranthis hyemalis
Gembos Yayla, S Anatolia
Dist: **S Anatolia**
J F **M A M** J J A S O N D

Eranthis longistipitata
Dzhabagly, Kazakhstan
Dist: **N and E Iran**
J F **M A M** J J A S O N D

Ranunculaceae: *Ranunculus*

Ranunculus asiaticus
Nr. Antakya, S Anatolia
Dist: S Anatolia and Islands
J F M **A** M J J A S O N D

Ranunculus ficaria ssp. calthifolia
Nr. Ibradi, S Anatolia
Dist: Scattered in Outer Anatolia
J F **M A** M J J A S O N D

Ranunculus kochii
Karabet Pass, SE Anatolia
Dist: E Anatolia
J F M **A M** J J A S O N D

Ranunculaceae: *Ranunculus*

Ranunculus myosuroides
Karabet Pass, SE Anatolia
Dist: S and SE Anatolia
J F M A M J **J A** S O N D

Ranunculus cadmicus
Cyprus
Dist: W and S Anatolia
J F M **A M J** J A S O N D

Ranunculus unguis-cati
Ahir Dağ, S Anatolia
Dist: Maraş Area, S Anatolia
J F M **A M** J J A S O N D

Berberidaceae

Two genera in the *Berberis* family have tuberous roots and these are *Bongardia and Leontice*.

Bongardia

There is only one species in the area, **Bongardia chrysogonum** **(Fig. 19)**, and this has very distinctive pinnate leaves with a reddish blotch at the base of the leaflets. The flowers are yellow and are usually found in fallow fields or cultivated ground in E Anatolia and N Iran. The plant illustrated is just coming into flower. It becomes much taller and more branched as it grows.

Leontice

The most widely distributed species is **Leontice leontopetalum** **(Fig. 20)** which grows widely in Anatolia and W Iran. It is a larger, much-branched plant with similar yellow flowers to *Bongardia* and is again found in cultivated fields. In Iran there is a second species **L. armenaica** (*L. minor*), which has larger flowers on unbranched stems, and this is illustrated in flower **(Fig. 21)** and with its inflated fruits **(Fig. 22)**.

Bongardia chrysogonum
Golestan, NE Iran
Dist: E Anatolia, Islands, N and W Iran
J F M **A M** J J A S O N D

Berberidaceae: *Leontice*

Leontice leontopetalum
Tooran, N Iran
Dist: Scattered in Mediterranean area, N and W Iran
J **F M A M** J J A S O N D

Fig 020

Fig 021

Leontice armenaica
Khonzar Pass, NW Iran
Dist: W Iran
J F **M A** M J J A S O N D

Leontice armenaica (fruit)
Nr. Chelgerd, W Iran
Dist: W Iran
J F **M A** M J J A S O N D

Fig 022

Fumariaceae

This is again a family with mostly 'non-bulbous' species, but many *Corydalis* species have tuberous roots and these are the ones covered here. There are about 20 species in the area and many are quite similar and difficult to tell apart, but their localised geographical distribution limits the choice.

Corydalis

There are several non-tuberous *Corydalis* species in the European area, but in Turkey and Iran only tuberous species are present.

Mountain Species with Bluish Flowers

Corydalis conorhiza (Fig. 23)
This is a glaucous-leaved species with bluish-purple flowers, that grows on stony mountain slopes in NE Anatolia.

Corydalis alpestris (Fig. 24)
This is another species from NE Anatolia with 5-8 bluish flowers in a tight inflorescence. As with *C. conorhiza* it usually grows at altitudes above 2,000m.

Mountain Species with Pink or White Flowers

Corydalis chionophylla (Fig. 25)
C. chionophylla is also an alpine species but this time from N Iran. It is very compact and short-stemmed with quite large, pinkish flowers, but a subspecies, **ssp. firouzii (Fig. 26)**, has yellow flowers which go red with age.

Corydalis oppositifolia (Figs. 27, 28)
There are two forms of *C. oppositifolia*, **ssp. oppositifolia** and **ssp. kurdica**. The former occurs on mountains in E Anatolia and the latter in similar situations in SE Anatolia and W Iran. The flower colour is white or pink turning red with age.

C. oppositifolia is part of a group of species, many of which were all included under the name of *C. rutifolia*. In this area the other species in the group are *C. erdelii, C. nariniana, C. verticillaris* and *C. lydica*.

Corydalis erdelii (Fig. 29)
This is a species with reddish-purple flowers found on mountains in S Anatolia. It has rather thick, very glaucous leaves.

Corydalis nariniana (Fig. 30)
This is a distinctive species with relatively large, white flowers with a purplish-red spur, which is largely recorded from E Anatolia. However the plant illustrated was on Davraz Dağ, near Eğridir in C Anatolia.

Corydalis verticillaris (Fig. 31)
This species is found on mountains in W and NW Iran. It has quite large pink flowers with a distinctive, strongly-recurved spur.

Corydalis lydica (not illustrated)
This is the only species from this group in W Anatolia, and is known particularly from Ulu Dağ near Bursa. It is a compact plant with creamy-white flowers.

Woodland and Lower Mountain Species from S Anatolia

Corydalis wendelboi (Fig. 32)
C. wendelboi represents another group of species that include *C. tauricola, C. paschei, C. angustifolia* and *C. haussknechtii*. *C. wendelboi* itself is an attractive species with an upright habit, bright green leaves and many small pink or red flowers. It is found in SW and S Anatolia amongst scrub or on mountain slopes.

Corydalis tauricola (Fig. 33)
This closely related species has fewer and larger white or pale pink flowers. It grows in deciduous woodland in the E Taurus and Amanus mountains.

Corydalis paschei (Fig. 34)
This species is only known from two small areas west of Antalya, and it has many, narrow, white to pale pink flowers.

Corydalis haussknechtii (not illustrated)
This is the only *Corydalis* in this group from SE Anatolia, where it grows in mountains in the Kurdish area. It has lax racemes of white flowers tipped with blackish-purple.

Corydalis angustifolia (Fig. 35)
This species has been found in NE Anatolia and is widely distributed in the Alborz mountains of N Iran. It has short, quite dense racemes of 2-10 white flowers and grows in forest and scrub habitats.

Very Localised Species in S Anatolia

Corydalis triternata (Fig. 36)
This delicate-looking, white to pale pink flowered species is only found in the Hatay district. The corolla is nodding and has a short spur.

Corydalis henrikii (Fig. 37)
This species is closely related to the previous one and is even more delicate having flowers with a very thin spur. It was found in 1990 on limestone screes in the Kartal Dağ range in Gaziantep province.

Species from NW Turkey

Corydalis caucasica (Fig. 38)
C. caucasica is, as its name suggests, mainly found in the Caucasus mountains, but a particular form, **ssp. abantensis**, has been found near Bolu in NW Turkey. It has dense racemes of pale lilac or white flowers and grows in beech scrub.

Corydalis integra (Fig. 40)
This is closely related to *C. caucasica* and is found in W Turkey and some of the Islands. It has erect stems with a dense, 8-20, pale pink flowered raceme, and grows on scrubby hillsides.

Corydalis marschalliana (Fig. 41)
This is a distinctive form of the widespread *C. bulbosa* with pale yellow flowers, which occurs in deciduous woodland in NW Turkey and N Iran.

Corydalis solida (Fig. 39)
This well-known European species occurs in scrub in many parts of Outer Anatolia. It has deeply divided bracts and pink or mauve racemes of flowers. *C. tauricola* is often considered as a subspecies of *C. solida*.

Fumariaceae: *Corydalis*

Corydalis alpestris
Ovit Dağ, NE Anatolia
Dist: NE Anatolia (Lazistan)
J F M A M J **J** A S O N D

Corydalis conorhiza
Anzer Valley, NE Anatolia
Dist: NE Anatolia (Lazistan)
J F M A M J **J** A S O N D

Corydalis chionophylla* ssp. *chionophylla
Khosh Yelagh, N Iran
Dist: N Iran
J F M **A M** J J A S O N D

Corydalis chionophylla* ssp. *firouzii
Olang, N Iran
Dist: N Iran
J F M **A M** J J A S O N D

Fumariaceae: *Corydalis*

***Corydalis oppositifolia*
ssp. *oppositifolia***
Çam Pass, NE Anatolia
Dist: E Anatolia
J F M **A M J** J A S O N D

Fig 027

Fig 028

***Corydalis oppositifolia*
ssp. *kurdica***
Nr. Alasht, W Iran
Dist: SE Anatolia, W Iran
J F M **A M J** J A S O N D

Corydalis erdelii
Ahir Dağ, Maraş, S Anatolia
Dist: Scattered, mainly in
C, S and E Anatolia
J F M **A M J** J A S O N D

Fig 029

Fumariaceae: *Corydalis*

Corydalis verticillaris
Nr. Khomeyn, N Iran
Dist: NW Iran
J F M **A M** J J A S O N D

Corydalis nariniana
Davraz Dağ, C Anatolia
Dist: Mainly E Anatolia
J F M **A M** J J A S O N D

Corydalis wendelboi
Püren Pass, Maraş, S Anatolia
Dist: W and S Anatolia
J F M **A M** J J A S O N D

Corydalis tauricola
Baskonus, Amanus Mts., S Anatolia
Dist: S Anatolia
J F M **A M** J J A S O N D

Fumariaceae: *Corydalis*

Corydalis paschei
In cultivation in the UK
Dist: SW Anatolia
J F **M A M** J J A S O N D

Fig 034

Corydalis angustifolia
Asalem Pass, N Iran
Dist: E Anatolia and N Iran
J F M **A M** J J A S O N D

Fig 035

Corydalis triternata
In cultivation in the UK
Dist: Taurus Mts., S Anatolia
J F M **A M** J J A S O N D

Fig 036

Fumariaceae: *Corydalis*

Corydalis henrikii
In cultivation in the UK
Dist: Gaziantep area,
S Anatolia
J F M **A** M J J A S O N D

Corydalis caucasica
In cultivation in the UK
Dist: Bolu, N Anatolia
J F M **A** M J J A S O N D

Corydalis solida
Nr. Akseki, S Anatolia
Dist: Outer Anatolia
J F M **A M** J J A S O N D

Fumariaceae: *Corydalis/Cyclamen*

Corydalis integra
In cultivation in the UK
Dist: W Turkey and Islands
J F **M A M** J J A S O N D

Corydalis marschalliana
Olang, N Iran
Dist: N Anatolia, N Iran
J F M **A M** J J A S O N D

Cyclamen coum, Lake Abant, N Anatolia

Primulaceae

The *Primula* family does not contain any bulbous species, but the one genus which does come within the scope of this book is *Cyclamen*. All species of *Cyclamen* grow from a corm, and these can live for many years and become large in size. Turkey has more species of *Cyclamen* than any other country and individual populations can be very extensive.

Cyclamen

The genus *Cyclamen* has always been popular with gardeners and flower enthusiasts, and many of the wild species come from this area. About twelve species occur, some in very large numbers. Both spring and autumn flowering species are present, and other important characteristics are the presence or absence of auricles (ear-like projections) at the base of the corolla, and the shape and time of appearance of the leaves.

Flowers with Distinct Auricles. Autumn Flowering

Cyclamen hederifolium (Figs. 43,44)
This species reaches the eastern limit of its distribution in W Turkey and is found in that area and on the Islands. It grows on shady slopes and banks and often has a very large tuber, which is distinctive in only producing roots from the top and sides. The flowers are white or pale pink and have a v-shaped crimson blotch at the base of the petals with two narrow points of colour extending a short way towards the tip. The variably shaped, angled leaves, which appear after the flowers, are coarsely toothed.

Cyclamen graecum (Figs. 45-48)
This similar species has beautifully marked heart-shaped leaves with toothed margins. They are very variable and usually appear after the flowers, but in more shady places both may be present. The flowers are pink or white with two larger and one smaller dark crimson

marks at the corolla base. They grow in hotter and drier sites than the previous species in pine forests, macchie and amongst limestone rocks.

Two subspecies occur in the area, **ssp. graecum** (**Fig. 45**) from the Islands with flowers having well developed auricles and basal markings extending along the veins, and **ssp. anatolicum** (**Fig. 46**) from SW Anatolia with less well developed auricles and short and blotchy markings.

Flowers without Auricles. Autumn Flowering

Cyclamen cilicium (Fig. 49)
This species comes from coniferous woodland in mountain areas of S Anatolia. It has long sharply-pointed petals which are deep pink or white with a conspicuous crimson blotch at the base and a somewhat constricted corolla mouth. The leaves appear with the flowers and are marbled and oval in shape.

Cyclamen intaminatum (Fig. 50)
This was originally described as a subspecies of *C. cilicium* but is now accepted as a separate species. It is a small plant with a small tuber, and the unmarked leaves, which appear earlier than with *C. cilicium*, are circular or kidney-shaped with scalloped edges. The flowers are similar to those of *C. cilicium*, but again they are smaller in size. They are white or pale pink in colour without any basal markings, and the corolla has an unconstricted mouth. It grows very locally in oak woods in NW Anatolia.

Cyclamen mirabile (Fig. 51)
This species is close to *C. cilicium*, but the easiest distinguishing feature is the irregularly toothed apex to the petals. The corolla is pale pink with darker basal blotches. The leaves are circular and often toothed with reddish marbling above, and some are present with the flowers. It grows in pine forests and macchie in SW Anatolia.

Flowers without Auricles. Spring Flowering

Cyclamen persicum (Fig. 52)
This is the largest flowered of the wild *Cyclamen* species, and is the parent of the commonly grown greenhouse *Cyclamen*. The flowers are large, white or pink, and have a purplish basal zone. The leaves are heart-shaped and are fully developed at flowering time. It grows in pine woodland, macchie and on stony slopes in W and S Anatolia and the Islands.

Cyclamen repandum ssp. *rhodense* (Fig. 53)
Cyclamen repandum is generally found in the central Mediterranean region, but an endemic form, *ssp. rhodense*, grows on the island of Rhodes . The flowers are white or pale pink with a poorly-defined, darker zone at the base. The heart-shaped leaves appear just before the flowers and often have a marbled upper surface, and the plant is usually found in pine forests on the island.

Cyclamen pseudibericum (Figs. 54,55)
This endemic *Cyclamen* is restricted to the Taurus and Amanus mountains in S Anatolia, and is found in pine woodland and beech scrub. The heart-shaped leaves appear before the flowers and are marbled and glossy. The corolla is bright magenta with a very conspicuous dark basal blotch.

Cyclamen coum (Figs. 42, 56–58)
This well-known species, which is grown in large numbers in cultivation, comes from Turkey-in-Europe and Outer Anatolia. The typical subspecies, *ssp. coum* (**Figs. 56, 57**) has relatively small, pale or dark magenta flowers, with a dark basal blotch surrounded by a pale eye. The **ssp. caucasicum** (**Fig. 58**) is found in N Anatolia and N and NW Iran. The leaves, which appear before the flowers, are circular and entire with *ssp. coum*, whereas the larger-flowered *ssp. caucasicum* has more heart-shaped, toothed leaves with a pointed apex.

Cyclamen alpinum (*C. trochopteranthum*) (Figs. 59–61)
The leaves of this species are like those of *C. coum*, but the lobes of the corolla are twisted so that they resemble the blades of a helicopter (**Fig. 61**). They are pale or deep pink in colour with a dark basal blotch, but without the white eye of *C. coum*. It is found in pine forests or on stony ground in SW Anatolia.

Cyclamen elegans (Figs. 62, 63)
This *Cyclamen* is endemic to northern Iran, occurring in the Caspian forests on the north side of the Alborz mountains. It is again similar to *C. coum* but the leaves are pointed and heart-shaped with a distinct, scalloped margin. The flowers are larger and have more pointed petals with pale to deep pink eyes.

Cyclamen parviflorum (Fig. 64)
The habitat of this *Cyclamen* is different to all others, as it is a high alpine species flowering in grassland close to melting snow in NE Anatolia. It has small, pale purple or pink flowers on short stems, and the round leaves are dark green and persist throughout the year.

Primulaceae: *Cyclamen*

Fig 043

Cyclamen hederifolium
Island of Lesbos
Dist: W Turkey, Islands
J F M A M J J **A S O N** D

Fig 044

Cyclamen hederifolium
Nr. Izmir, W Turkey
Dist: W Turkey, Islands
J F M A M J J **A S O N** D

Fig 045

Cyclamen graecum ssp. graecum
Island of Lesbos
Dist: Islands
J F M A M J J A **S O N** D

Fig 046

Cyclamen graecum ssp. anatolicum
Finike, S Anatolia
Dist: SW and S Anatolia
J F M A M J J A **S O N** D

Primulaceae: *Cyclamen*

Cyclamen graecum
Phaselis, S Anatolia
Dist: SW and S Anatolia, Islands
J F M A M J J A **S O N D**

Fig 047

Fig 048

Cyclamen graecum
Phaselis, S Anatolia
Dist: SW and S Anatolia, Islands
J F M A M J J A **S O N D**

Cyclamen cilicium
Finike, S Anatolia
Dist: S Anatolia
J F M A M J J A **S O N D**

Fig 049

Primulaceae: *Cyclamen*

Cyclamen intaminatum
Bilecik, NW Anatolia
Dist: NW Anatolia
J F M A M J J A **S O N** D

Cyclamen mirabile
Tahtali Dağ, S Anatolia
Dist: SW Anatolia
J F M A M J J A **S O N** D

Cyclamen persicum
Island of Chios
Dist: W and S Anatolia, Islands
J **F M A** M J J A S O N D

Cyclamen repandum ssp. rhodense
Island of Rhodes
Dist: Rhodes
J F **M A M** J J A S O N D

Primulaceae: *Cyclamen*

Cyclamen pseudibericum
Nr. Gaziantep, S Anatolia
Dist: S Anatolia
J F **M A M** J J A S O N D

Cyclamen pseudibericum
Nr. Gaziantep, S Anatolia
Dist: S Anatolia
J F **M A M** J J A S O N D

Cyclamen coum ssp. coum
Lake Abant, N Anatolia
Dist: Turkey-in-Europe, Outer Anatolia
J **F M A M** J J A S O N D

Cyclamen coum ssp. coum
In cultivation in the UK
Dist: Turkey-in-Europe, Outer Anatolia
J **F M A M** J J A S O N D

Cyclamen coum ssp. caucasicum
Nr. Masuleh, NW Iran
Dist: N Iran
J **F M A M** J J A S O N D

Primulaceae: *Cyclamen*

Cyclamen alpinum
Ölüdeniz, SW Anatolia
Dist: SW Anatolia
J **F M A** M J J A S O N D

Cyclamen alpinum
Sinekçibeli Pass, SW Anatolia
Dist: SW Anatolia
J **F M A** M J J A S O N D

Cyclamen alpinum
In cultivation in the UK
Dist: SW Anatolia
J **F M A** M J J A S O N D

Cyclamen elegans
From Rasht, N Iran
Dist: N Iran
J F M A M J J A S O N D

Cyclamen elegans
Rasht, N Iran
Dist: N Iran
J F M A M J J A S O N D

Cyclamen parviflorum
Zigana Pass, NE Anatolia
Dist: NE Anatolia
J F M **A M J** J A S O N D

Araceae:

Dracunculus vulgaris, Rhodes

Araceae

This family is distinguished by the unusual form of its flowers which consist of a central spike (the spadix) surrounded by a large bract (the spathe) which can be leaf-like or petal-like. The spadix is elongated into a long, cylindrical, club-shaped appendix which is usually purple or yellow in colour. At the base of this are a ring of female flowers and above them a ring of male flowers. The form of these is often a diagnostic feature as well as the colour and form of the spathe and spadix. The leaves are all basal, and the fruits are in the form of a cluster of berries, often red in colour.

Arum

This is the largest genus in the family in this area and covers the typical 'cuckoo-pints' of the European region. Most species grow in shady places.

Arum italicum (Fig. 66)

This species is well-known to gardeners, and is widespread in the Mediterranean and Southern European regions. It has a large yellow-green spathe and a yellow spadix. The leaves are large and have the typical spear-shaped form, and in Turkey do not have the white veins present in some forms. The plant occurs in N Turkey and NW Iran growing amongst shrubs and in disturbed situations. It has bright red berries in the autumn **(Fig. 67)**.

Arum nickelii (Fig. 68)

This species also has a greenish spathe, often with a brownish edge, and the large, brownish or greenish-yellow spadix is about half the length of the spathe. Botanically it is separated from *A. italicum* on the basis of differences in the sterile zones above the flowers. It grows on shady banks and streamsides in W Anatolia and the Islands.

Arum maculatum (Fig. 69)

This familiar species has a pale green spathe and a dark purple spadix, and the tube of the spathe is whitish with a purple band across the centre. The large leaves are distinctive in usually having dark blotches or spots over their surface. It is found in N Turkey, W Anatolia and the Islands, and grows in woods or scrub or on shady slopes.

Arum orientale (Fig. 70)

This species is similar to *A. nickelii* but the outside of the spathe is slightly purplish and sometimes has a purplish edge. The tube has a purple ring in the middle like *A. maculatum* but the leaves are unspotted. The spadix is slender and red-grey to blackish-grey in colour. It grows in damp, shady valleys in N Anatolia and N Iran.

Arum detruncatum (Figs. 71,72)

Arum detruncatum, *A. elongatum* and *A. conophalloides* have been a confusing group in Turkey and this has been resolved in the revision in Vol. 10 of the Flora. It seems that species previously described as *A. elongatum ssp. detruncatum* and *A. conophalloides* are both varieties of *A. detruncatum*.

Arum detruncatum has three recognised varieties, **v. virescens (Fig. 71)**, **v. caudatum** (*not illustrated*) and **v. detruncatum (Fig. 72)**. The *virescens* form has a green spathe, which is only purple on the margin, and the spadix is yellowish brown. The other two varieties both have purple-brown spathes and a purple spadix. The difference is that *v. caudatum* has a spathe that is broadest at about the middle point, and with *v. detruncatum* the spathe is broadest near the base. The latter is the *A. conophalloides* form. All varieties grow on rocky slopes and in steppe and scrub, and the species has been found in Inner Anatolia and N Iran.

Arum dioscoridis (Figs. 73–76)

This is a very variable species and five varieties are recognised. All forms have purple spots on the inside of the spathe but these markings vary a great deal. The most spectacular form is **v. spectabile (Fig. 73)** with a spathe which is almost completely stained purple. The spadix is blackish-violet, and this form occurs in SW Anatolia and NW Iran. It also grows on the island of Cyprus.

In the Amanus and Mesopotamian regions the form present is **v. syriaca (Fig. 75)**, and this has a greenish spathe with most purple spots in the lower half.

Other varieties which have a pink or purplish inside to the top of the tube include **v. liepoldtii (Fig. 76)** from W and S Anatolia and islands such as Rhodes, and **v. luschanii** from S Anatolia. All grow on rocky hillsides, field edges and roadsides.

Arum creticum (Fig. 77)

This very distinctive *Arum* is found mainly on the island of Crete, but it has also been reported from SW Anatolia and islands such as Samos. The Cretan form has a large yellow or cream spathe which rapidly folds back to disclose the prominent, yellow spadix. Turkish forms apparently have a larger spathe and an even larger spadix, and they grow on rocky hillsides.

Other species found in Turkey include *A. elongatum*, *A. byzantinum*, *A. euxinum* and *A. balansanum*.

Araceae: *Arum*

Arum italicum
Nr. Trabzon, N Anatolia
Dist: N Anatolia
J F M **A M** J J A S O N D

Arum italicum (fruit)
Nr. Trabzon, N Anatolia
Dist: N Anatolia
J F M **A M** J J A S O N D

Arum nickelii
Island of Chios
Dist: W Anatolia, Islands
J F M **A M** J J A S O N D

Arum maculatum
Nr. Istanbul, N Turkey
Dist: N Turkey, W Anatolia, Islands
J F M **A M** J J A S O N D

Araceae: *Arum*

Arum orientale
Ordu, N Anatolia
Dist: N Anatolia, N Iran
J F **M A M** J J A S O N D

Arum detruncatum v. virescens
Nr. Bitlis, SE Anatolia
Dist: Inner Anatolia, N Iran
J F M A **M J** J A S O N D

Arum detruncatum v. detruncatum
Bagoran, Inner Anatolia
Dist: Inner Anatolia, N and NW Iran
J F M A **M J** J A S O N D

Arum dioscoridis v. spectabile
Perge, SW Anatolia
Dist: SW Anatolia, NW Iran
J F **M A M** J J A S O N D

Araceae: *Arum*

Arum dioscoridis* v. *dioscoridis
N Cyprus
Dist: SW Anatolia
J F **M A M** J J A S O N D

Arum dioscoridis* v. *syriaca
Nr. Maraş, S Anatolia
Dist: S Anatolia
J F **M A M** J J A S O N D

Arum dioscoridis* v. *liepoldtii
Island of Rhodes
Dist: SW Anatolia, Islands
J F **M A M** J J A S O N D

Arum creticum
Crete
Dist: SW Anatolia, Island of Samos
J F **M A M** J J A S O N D

Araceae: *Biarum*

Biarum

This genus is similar to *Arum* but the spathes are generally smaller and often brown in colour. They are initially erect but often become recurved with age. The spadix has a long appendage. The leaves are simple in shape and appear after the flowers.

Biarum tenuifolium (Figs. 78,79)

This spring-flowering species has an erect, deep brown spathe which is greenish outside. The spadix is also brown, slightly hooked at the tip, and somewhat longer than the spathe. The leaves are not present at flowering time, and the plant grows in rocky ground and macchie in SW Anatolia and on the Islands.

Biarum davisii ssp. *marmarisensis* (Fig. 80)

This very distinctive *Biarum* is autumn-flowering, again often without the leaves. The spathe is whitish and suffused with purple-brown, and it curves forward over the reddish-brown spadix. The outside is pale green with faint purple mottling. The **ssp. davisii (Fig. 81)** occurs only in Crete, but the Turkish form, ssp. *marmarisensis*, is more robust with a larger spathe. It grows in rocky places in SW Anatolia in the Muğla and Marmaris areas.

Biarum eximium (Fig. 82)

This is another autumn-flowering species with a spathe that is purple outside and dark purple inside, and it quickly curves back. The brown spadix is slightly shorter than the spathe. It grows at low levels in S Anatolia.

***Biarum pyrami* (Fig. 83)** is a very similar species from the Antalya area of S Anatolia, but in this case the spadix is much longer than the spathe and the whole plant is relatively large.

Biarum bovei (Fig. 84)

This is a similar but rather smaller species with a brownish-purple spathe and a brown spadix. It is found in macchie and fields in Inner and S Anatolia.

Biarum ditschianum (Fig. 85)

This unmistakeable species is endemic to Turkey and is known only from the Eşen River Valley in Antalya. It has a greatly reduced spathe which is greenish outside and purplish inside, and a stout yellow spadix which is the dominant feature of the plant. It flowers in the spring in crevices in limestone rocks.

The other species present in Turkey is *Biarum carduchorum* from S and E Anatolia. This species also occurs in SW Iran, together with the endemic *Biarum straussii*.

Fig 078

Biarum tenuifolium
Island of Rhodes
Dist: SW Anatolia, Islands
J F M **A M** J J A S O N D

Araceae: *Biarum*

Biarum tenuifolium
Greece
Dist: SW Anatolia, Islands
J F **M A M J** J A S O N D

Biarum davisii* ssp. *marmarisensis
From Muğla, SW Anatolia
Dist: SW Anatolia
J F M A M J J A S **O** N D

Biarum davisii* ssp. *davisii
Crete
Dist: Crete
J F M A M J J A S **O** N D

Biarum eximium
Nr. Feke, S Anatolia
Dist: S Anatolia (Taurus)
J F M A M J J A **S** O N D

49

Araceae: *Biarum*

Biarum pyrami
Nr. Antalya, S Anatolia
Dist: S Anatolia
J F M A M J J A **S O N D**

Biarum bovei
Nr. Antalya, S Anatolia
Dist: Inner and S Anatolia
J F M A M J J A S O **N D**

Biarum ditschianum
Nr. Dalaman, S Anatolia
Dist: S Anatolia (Antalya)
J F M A **M J** J A S O N D

Araceae: *Eminium*

Eminium

This is a genus of spring-flowering species which generally have 3-lobed leaves that are largely developed at flowering time. The spadix is short and cylindrical or conical in shape.

Eminium spiculatum (Fig. 86)
This species has a spathe which is purple-spotted on the outside and blackish-purple on the inside. The leaf stems are also purple-spotted, and the spadix is dark purple. It occurs in stony steppe and fields in the Gaziantep area of S Anatolia. The spathe has withered on the illustrated plant.

Eminium rauwolffii (Fig. 87)
This species has a spathe which is green outside and maroon inside, and the edges of the spathe usually curve inwards above the blackish-purple spadix. The leaf stems are not purple-spotted. It grows on stony hillsides and in fields in S and E Anatolia.

Eminium intortum (Fig. 88)
A closely related species, which is often confused with *E. rauwolffii*, is *E. intortum*, which is found in SW Iran and possibly in SE Anatolia. They differ in the flower stem being thickened below the spathe in *E. rauwolffii* but not with *E. intortum*, and there are differences in leaf form and veining.

Eminium koenenianum (Fig. 89)
This differs from all other species in having entire leaves with distinct white patches on them. It comes from dry, rocky slopes in the Çoruh Valley of NE Anatolia. The spathe is brownish-violet on the outside and dark violet on the inside, and the spadix is blackish-brown.

Eminium spiculatum
Nr Gaziantep, S Anatolia
Dist: S Anatolia (Gaziantep)
J F M **A M** J J A S O N D

Eminium rauwolffii
Nr. Mardin, SE Anatolia
Dist: S and E Anatolia
J F **M A M** J J A S O N D

Eminium intortum
Nr. Shulabad, W Iran
Dist: W Iran
J F M **A M** J J A S O N D

Eminium koenenianum
Çoruh Valley, NE Anatolia
Dist: NE Anatolia
J F M **A** M J J A S O N D

Araceae: *Arisarum/Dracunculus*

Arisarum

There is only one species of this genus in our area **Arisarum vulgare (Fig. 90)**. This has a wide distribution in the Mediterranean region and is found in W and S Anatolia and on the Islands. It flowers in the winter and early spring, and has a pale to dark green striped spathe and a greenish or brownish spadix. The spear-shaped leaves have purple-spotted stems. It grows in shady places amongst oak scrub and macchie and on rocky hillsides.

Dracunculus

This is again a genus with a single species in the area, but it is by far the largest representative of the *Arum* family here. It has a very large, dark purple spathe which can be up to 50cm long, and a similarly coloured spadix. The leaves are kidney-shaped in outline and are divided into 9-13 narrow segments, and the sheath is purple-spotted. **Dracunculus vulgaris (Fig. 65, 91)** is widespread in the eastern Mediterranean and occurs in NW Turkey, W and C Anatolia and the Islands. It grows in field margins and other disturbed habitats at low altitudes.

Arisarum vulgare
Island of Lesbos
Dist: W and S Anatolia, Islands
J F **M A M** J J A S O N D

Dracunculus vulgaris
Island of Rhodes
Dist: NW Turkey, W and C Anatolia, Islands
J F M **A M** J J A S O N D

Asphodelaceae

This is one of several families that have been separated from the original *Liliaceae* family. All members of these families have flowers with six stamens and a superior ovary. The *Asphodelaceae* are the group that perhaps fit least comfortably in a 'bulbous' book, but many are rhizomatous perennials with thickened roots. The family includes *Asphodelus*, *Eremurus*, *Asphodeline* and *Anthericum*.

Asphodelus

The asphodels are very familiar in the Mediterranean region, and three species are present in Turkey and one in Iran.

Asphodelus fistulosus (Figs. 92,93)
This species is up to 60cm tall and usually forms clumps with a branched and rather lax inflorescence of white or pale pink flowers with a brownish central vein on the tepals. It grows in stony places and in fallow fields in W and S Anatolia and the Islands.

Asphodelus aestivus (Figs. 94,95)
This is a much larger plant, up to 2m tall, with a strongly branched, dense inflorescence. The flowers are similar to those of *A. fistulosus* and are white with a pinkish or brownish central vein. It grows in fields at low levels in NW Turkey, W and S Anatolia and the Islands.

The third species is *A. ramosus* which differs from *A. aestivus* in its larger seed capsules and larger perianth segments. It has been recorded in NW Anatolia. The species found in W Iran is *A. tenuifolius* which is a relatively small annual plant related to *A. fistulosus*.

Asphodelaceae: *Asphodelus*

Fig 092

Asphodelus fistulosus
Island of Rhodes
Dist: W and S Anatolia, Islands
J F **M A M** J J A S O N D

Fig 093

Asphodelus fistulosus
Island of Rhodes
Dist: W and S Anatolia, Islands
J F **M A M** J J A S O N D

Fig 094

Asphodelus aestivus
Island of Chios
Dist: NW Turkey, W and S Anatolia, Islands
J F **M A M** J J A S O N D

Fig 095

Asphodelus aestivus
Island of Rhodes
Dist: NW Turkey, W and S Anatolia, Islands
J F **M A M** J J A S O N D

Asphodelaceae: *Eremurus*

Eremurus

These tall, asphodel-like plants are most commonly found beyond the east of our area. However, seven species are found in Iran and two, at the western limit of their range, in Turkey. All the species have a rosette of basal leaves and a leafless stem, and they are often dominant where they occur.

Eremurus spectabilis (Figs. 96,97)
This species is up to 1.5m tall and has greenish-yellow flowers with prominent orange anthers. It grows in dry steppe and in open, rocky scrub on hillsides in Inner Anatolia.

Eremurus persicus (Fig. 98)
This is a smaller plant up to 70cm tall with white or pale pink flowers with reflexed tepals. It grows on dry, rocky slopes in NW and W Iran.

Eremurus luteus (Fig. 99)
This species grows up to 1m tall and has pale, greenish-yellow flowers with a darker yellow stripe in the centre of the tepals. The pedicels are relatively long (up to 35mm), and the plants grow in dry, bare ground in N and W Iran.

Eremurus kopetdaghensis (Figs. 100,101)
This smaller species is up to 65cm tall with narrow leaves (3-6mm) and white flowers with a yellow base and a pale brown central vein on the tepals. It grows on dry, stony hillsides in N and W Iran.

Eremurus olgae (Fig. 102)
This species is similar to *E. kopetdaghensis* but has broader leaves (up to 15mm) and a taller flower spike (up to 1m) of white to pale rose-coloured flowers with a yellow base. It is found on open, stony ground and occurs widely in Iran.

Eremurus stenophyllus (Figs. 103,104)
This is a very striking, yellow-flowered *Eremurus* with stems up to 1.5m, and a dense raceme of flowers. It is found on stony hillsides in C and E Iran.

Other *Eremurus* present are two closely related species *E. cappadocicus* in E Anatolia and *E. inderiensis* with a widespread distribution in Iran.

Fig 096
Eremurus spectabilis
Lake Van, SE Anatolia
Dist: Inner Anatolia
J F M A **M J J** A S O N D

Fig 097
Eremurus spectabilis
Nr. Semirom, W Iran
Dist: Inner Anatolia
J F M A **M J J** A S O N D

Asphodelaceae: *Eremurus*

Eremurus persicus
Nr. Miyaneh, W Iran
Dist: NW and W Iran
J F M A **M J** J A S O N D

Eremurus luteus
Nr. Tehran, N Iran
Dist: N and W Iran
J F M **A M** J J A S O N D

Eremurus kopetdaghensis
Golestan, NE Iran
Dist: N and W Iran
J F M **A M** J J A S O N D

Eremurus kopetdaghensis
Golestan, NE Iran
Dist: N and W Iran
J F M **A M** J J A S O N D

Asphodelaceae: *Eremurus*

Eremurus olgae
Nr. Takt e Suleyman, W Iran
Dist: W, N and E Iran
J F M **A M** J J A S O N D

Eremurus stenophyllus
Sabzak Pass, Afghanistan
Dist: C and E Iran
J F M **A M** J J A S O N D

Eremurus stenophyllus
In cultivation in the UK
Dist: C and E Iran
J F M **A M** J J A S O N D

Asphodelaceae: *Asphodeline*

Asphodeline

There are about 15 species in this genus in the area, most of them in Turkey. They have white or yellow flowers and leafy stems and many species have branched inflorescences.

Flowers yellow

Asphodeline lutea (Figs. 105,106)
This is the most familiar species as it is common over the whole Mediterranean region. It grows in Turkey-in-Europe, Outer Anatolia and the Islands, and is found on stony slopes in macchie and scrub. It is about 1m tall and is leafy all the way up the stem, with a dense head of starry, yellow flowers.

Asphodeline liburnica (Fig. 107)
This is similar to *A. lutea* but is a more delicate-looking plant with leaves only up to the middle of the stem. Again the flowers are yellow and starry, but the inflorescence is more lax. It is found in macchie and open forest in Turkey-in-Europe and the Islands.

Two other yellow-flowered species occur, *A. baytopae*, with long branches to the inflorescence, from S Anatolia, and *A. brevicaulis*, with a simple or branched flower spike, from W and S Anatolia.

Flowers white

Asphodeline taurica (Fig. 108)
This asphodel has an unbranched inflorescence which is leafy throughout. It grows in dry, rocky places in Inner Anatolia and is up to 80cm tall with glaucous leaves.

Asphodeline damascena (Figs. 109,110)
This is a branched, white-flowered asphodel, also from Inner Anatolia, and the stem is leafy to about three-quarters of its length. The form shown, **ssp. ovoidea**, is a local form from the Maraş area of S Anatolia, where it occurs on open, stony hillsides. Other forms are widespread in Anatolia.

All the other species in Turkey, and the two species in Iran, have white flowers and often branched inflorescences. Differences in the fruiting capsules often provide the distinguishing features.

Asphodeline lutea
Island of Rhodes
Dist: Turkey-in-Europe, Outer Anatolia, Islands
J F **M A M J** J A S O N D

Asphodeline lutea
Island of Lesbos
Dist: Turkey-in-Europe, Outer Anatolia, Islands
J F **M A M J** J A S O N D

Asphodelaceae: *Asphodeline*

Asphodeline liburnica
In cultivation in the UK
Dist: Turkey-in-Europe, Islands

Asphodeline taurica
Ala Dağ, Inner Anatolia
Dist: Inner Anatolia

Asphodeline damascena ssp. ovoidea
Ahir Dağ, Maraş, S Anatolia
Dist: S Anatolia (Maraş)

Asphodeline damascena ssp. ovoidea
Ahir Dağ, Maraş, S Anatolia
Dist: S Anatolia (Maraş)

Asphodelaceae: *Anthericum*

Anthericum

Two species of *Anthericum* are present in Turkey, both coming from the European element of the flora. Both have white asphodel-like flowers.

Anthericum liliago (Fig. 111)
This 60cm tall species has a simple, lax inflorescence with quite large, starry, white flowers. It grows in open woodland and grassy meadows in S Anatolia.

Anthericum ramosum (Fig. 112)
This taller species has a branched inflorescence and smaller, white flowers, and grows on calcareous hills in N Anatolia.

Anthericum liliago
Nr. Adana, S Anatolia
Dist: S Anatolia
J F M A M **J J** A S O N D

Anthericum ramosum
Nr. Safranbolu, N Anatolia
Dist: N Anatolia
J F M A M **J J** A S O N D

Alliaceae

The onion family is very large in both Turkey and Iran and is the most complex in the area. All are bulbous perennials with sheathing leaves and a terminal umbel of flowers, which is enclosed within a spathe when in bud. Most species smell of garlic or onion. The family includes *Allium* and *Nectaroscordum*.

Allium

Allium is a very complicated genus in this area as there are about 150 species in Turkey and 140 species in Iran. It needs a book of its own to cover such a range, so this account concentrates on a few species from each of the main sections into which *Allium* is divided.

Important factors in identification are the leaf form, shape and structure (solid or hollow), the colour and form of the perianth segments, the colour of stamens, the presence or absence of bulbils, and the bulb and bulb tunic. This group is difficult for the trained botanist and almost impossible for most of us, and the variation occurring with situation and altitude in this area only increases the problems.

Section Rhiziridium

This is a small section with only a few species.

Allium hymenorrhizum (Fig. 113)
This pink-flowered species has been recorded from the Mazandaran area of N Iran, and it grows in wet alpine meadows.

Allium albidum ssp. caucasicum (Fig. 114)
This species is white-flowered and it has a 10-30cm stem and a many-flowered, hemispherical umbel. It is found rarely on dry, south-facing slopes in NE Anatolia.

Allium schoenoprasum (Fig. 115)
The familiar 'chives' is found in E Anatolia growing by streams in alpine pastures and near melting snow.

Alliaceae: *Allium*

Section Cepa

There is only one species in the area in this section.

Allium cepa (Fig. 116)
This is the cultivated onion and it is widely grown in Turkey. It sometimes becomes naturalised, but its wild origin is not known for certain. It has a spherical head of white flowers.

Section Molium

This includes many well-known Mediterranean species.

Allium subhirsutum (Fig. 117)
This small, white-flowered species occurs in macchie and phrygana in SW Anatolia and on the Islands.

Allium trifoliatum (Fig. 118)
This is another small, white-flowered *Allium* but the flowers have a pink midvein to the tepals and they tend to go pink as they age. It is found in shady places and on stony ground in S Anatolia and on the Islands.

Allium neapolitanum (Fig. 119)
This is a larger, white-flowered species which is widely distributed in the Mediterranean region. It grows in macchie and phrygana, often in shady places, in Turkey-in-Europe, W and S Anatolia and the Islands.

Allium roseum (Fig. 120)
This is another common Mediterranean species which has distinctive pink flowers, and it grows in a wide range of habitats in NW and W Turkey, S and E Anatolia and on the Islands.

Section Briseis

There are only two species in this section.

Allium triquetrum (Fig. 121)
This *Allium* has been found naturalised in woodland in Turkey-in-Europe in the Istanbul area. It has a distinctive triangular stem and pendulous white flowers.

Allium paradoxum (Fig. 122)
This is another pendulous-flowered, white species which is very distinctive. The flowers are globular in shape, and the plant is found in deciduous woodland in N Iran.

Section Porphyroprason

There is only one species in this section.

Allium oreophilum (Figs. 123, 124)
This bright, pink-flowered species is sold within the nursery trade as *A. ostrowskianum*. It is found in rocky places in E Anatolia and also occurs in Afghanistan, but surprisingly has not been recorded in Iran.

Section Brevispatha

This is quite a small group.

Allium callidictyon (*A. fimbriatum*) (Fig. 125)
This short-stemmed *Allium* has a lax, few-flowered umbel of pinkish flowers with a green midvein. It grows in oak scrub, steppe or on rocky slopes in Inner Anatolia and NW Iran.

Allium callimischon ssp. haemostictum (Fig. 126)
This species has white or pale pink, cup-shaped flowers with a reddish midvein and reddish dots on the upper part of the tepals. It is found rarely in the Muğla area of S Anatolia.

Section Scorodon

This is one of the larger sections of the genus.

Allium balansae (Fig. 127)
This short-stemmed species has a hemispherical umbel of bell-shaped, rose-purple flowers. It grows on stony mountain slopes or scree in N and E Anatolia.

Allium rubellum (Fig. 128)
This pink-flowered species has tepals with a darker midvein and it grows in *Artemesia* steppe in the Doğubayazit area of E Anatolia. It is also widespread in N and NW Iran.

Section Codonoprasum

This is one of the largest sections in the genus.

Allium flavum (Fig. 129)
This species is yellow-flowered and there are different subspecies and varieties recognised in Turkey. The various forms are widely distributed from Turkey-in-Europe and the Islands to Outer Anatolia.

Allium carinatum ssp. pulchellum (Fig. 130)
This species is similar in appearance to *A. flavum* but the flowers are purple in colour. It grows in rocky places in the Çanakkale region of NW Turkey.

Allium stamineum (Fig. 131)
This *Allium* has pinkish-purple flowers which point downwards. The pedicels are very unequal giving an umbel shape to the flower head. It grows on dry, stony slopes in Turkey-in-Europe, W and S Anatolia and the Islands, and in N and W Iran.

Allium kurtzianum (Fig. 132)
This rare endemic *Allium* has a dense, many-flowered, hemispherical umbel of pinkish-purple,

bell-shaped flowers with a darker midvein. It is found on mountain slopes on marble in the Çanakkale region of NW Turkey.

Allium myrianthum (Fig. 133)
This species has cream or white, bell-shaped flowers in a many-flowered umbel. It grows in a wide range of habitats in W, S and C Anatolia, and in W Iran.

Section Allium
This is probably the largest of the sections.

Allium ampeloprasum (Fig. 134)
The wild leek is a tall plant (up to 1.8m) with a round head of usually purple flowers, with a green midvein on the tepals. It occurs in rocky steppe, scrub or by roadsides in Turkey-in-Europe, Outer Anatolia and the Islands, and in W Iran.

Allium junceum (Fig. 135)
This species has a tight head of purple flowers, and it is found on rocky slopes and scree in SW and S Anatolia and the Islands.

Allium guttatum (Fig. 136)
This species also has a tight head of flowers but they are usually whitish with a green or pink median stripe. It grows in oak scrub and pinewoods in NW Turkey, Anatolia and the Islands.

Section Acanthoprason
This is quite a large group of generally short-stemmed species in this area.

Allium akaka (Fig. 137)
This short-stemmed *Allium* has two broad leaves and an umbel of purplish-pink flowers with a darker midvein. It grows on dry, rocky slopes in E Anatolia and NW Iran.

Allium cristophii (*A. albipilosum*) (Figs. 138,139)
This very familiar garden *Allium* comes from C Anatolia, where it is rare, and N, E and C Iran. It is another plant of rocky hillsides, but has a very large head of small, starry, dull-purple flowers on a stem up to 60cm tall.

Allium shelkovnikovii (Fig. 140)
This species is similar to *A. akaka* with a short stem and a many-flowered umbel of purple flowers with a darker central vein on the tepals. It is restricted to stony hillsides in NW Iran.

Allium bodeanum (Fig. 141)
This *Allium* is closely related to *A. cristophii*, but it has a shorter stem, a tighter head of darker purple flowers and 1-3 broad leaves which are held close to the ground. It is endemic to E Iran, and is restricted to stony hillsides in the Gorgan and Khorasan regions.

Allium derderianum (Fig. 142)
This is another short-stemmed *Allium* with two, fairly broad leaves which are prostrate on the ground. It has an umbel of starry, pale purple flowers and is another endemic species, and it grows in N and C Iran.

Section Melanocrommyum
This is the final group and is again quite large.

Allium nigrum (Fig. 143)
This is a widespread Mediterranean species often growing in cultivated ground or on rocky slopes. It has a large, relatively flat umbel of pink flowers with a prominent green or purple ovary. It is about 1m tall and is found in Turkey-in-Europe, W and S Anatolia and on the Islands.

Allium cardiostemon (Fig. 144)
This species has a tight, spherical head of dark maroon flowers on a 30-60cm stem. It grows in steppe, scrub or on open rocky slopes in E Anatolia and NW Iran.

Allium orientale (Fig. 145)
This *Allium* has a 30-50cm stem bearing a flattish umbel of white or yellowish-white flowers with an obvious blackish-green or purple ovary. It is found in S and C Anatolia growing on rocky hills and slopes, often on limestone.

Allium kharputense (Fig. 146)
This is a species closely related to *A. orientale* but the tepals are narrower and they become reflexed at an early stage. It again has white or cream flowers and grows in fallow or cultivated land and on grassy slopes in E and S Anatolia, and in NW Iran.

Allium hirtifolium (Fig. 147)
This species is characterised by its 4-5 hairy leaves. It has a tall stem (up to 1.2m) with a large, spherical umbel of starry, purple flowers. It is found on rocky slopes in SE Anatolia, and is widely distributed in Iran.

Allium noëanum (Fig. 148)
This is another species from SE Anatolia and W and C Iran, and it has a 20-30cm stem and a hemispherical umbel of pink to mauve, bell-shaped flowers. It grows on clayey soils in cultivated land.

Alliaceae: *Allium*

Allium hymenorrhizum
Markakol, E Kazakhstan
Dist: N Iran (Mazandaran)
J F M A M **J J A** S O N D

Allium albidum* ssp. *caucasicum
Lake Çildir, NE Anatolia
Dist: NE Anatolia (rare)
J F M A M **J J A** S O N D

Allium schoenoprasum
Nr. Erzurum, E Anatolia
Dist: E Anatolia
J F M A M **J J A** S O N D

Allium cepa
N Greece
Dist: Cultivated
J F M A M **J J A** S O N D

Alliaceae: *Allium*

Allium subhirsutum
Island of Rhodes
Dist: SW Anatolia, Islands
J F **M A M** J J A S O N D

Allium trifoliatum
Island of Lesbos
Dist: S Anatolia, Islands
J F **M A M** J J A S O N D

Allium neapolitanum
Island of Chios
Dist: Turkey-in-Europe, W and S Anatolia, Islands
J F **M A M** J J A S O N D

Allium roseum
Island of Rhodes
Dist: NW and W Turkey, S and E Anatolia, Islands
J F **M A M** J J A S O N D

Alliaceae: *Allium*

Allium triquetrum
Cornwall, England
Dist: Turkey-in-Europe (naturalised)
J F M A M **J** J A S O N D

Allium paradoxum
Golestan, NE Iran
Dist: N Iran
J F M **A M** J J A S O N D

Allium oreophilum
Başkale, SE Anatolia
Dist: E Anatolia
J F M A M J **J** A S O N D

Allium oreophilum
In cultivation in the UK
Dist: E Anatolia
J F M A M J **J** A S O N D

Alliaceae: *Allium*

Allium callidictyon
From Ahir Dağ, Inner Anatolia
Dist: Inner Anatolia, NW Iran
J F M A M J **J A** S O N D

Allium callimischon* ssp. *haemostictum
From Muğla, SW Anatolia
Dist: SW Anatolia (rare)
J F M A M J J A **S O** N D

Allium balansae
From Erzurum, E Anatolia
Dist: N and E Anatolia
J F M A M J J **A** S O N D

Allium rubellum
Alborz Mts., N Iran
Dist: NW Turkey, E Anatolia, N and NW Iran
J F M A **M J J A** S O N D

Allium flavum
Özhatay, Turkey-in-Europe
Dist: Turkey-in-Europe, Outer Anatolia, Islands
J F M A **M J J A** S O N D

Alliaceae: *Allium*

Allium carinatum* ssp. *pulchellum
In cultivation at RBG Edinburgh
Dist: Turkey-in-Europe, NW Turkey
J F M A M **J J A S** O N D

Allium stamineum
Nr. Biriçek, S Anatolia
Dist: Turkey-in-Europe, W and S Anatolia, Islands, N and W Iran
J F M A M **J J A S** O N D

Allium kurtzianum
From Çanakkale, NW Turkey
Dist: NW Turkey (Çanakkale, rare)
J F M A M J **J** A S O N D

Allium myrianthum
Nr. Osmaniye, S Anatolia
Dist: W, S and C Anatolia, W Iran
J F M A M **J J** A S O N D

Alliaceae: *Allium*

Allium ampeloprasum
Island of Rhodes
Dist: Turkey-in-Europe, Outer Anatolia, Islands
J F M A **M J** J A S O N D

Allium junceum
Cyprus
Dist: SW Anatolia, Islands
J F M **A M** J J A S O N D

Allium guttatum
Nr. Çanakkale, NW Turkey
Dist: NW Turkey, Anatolia, Islands
J F M A M J **J A S** O N D

Allium akaka
Güzeldere Pass, SE Anatolia
Dist: E Anatolia, NW Iran
J F M A **M J** J A S O N D

Allium cristophii
Golestan, N Iran
Dist: C Anatolia, N, E and C Iran
J F M A **M J** J A S O N D

Alliaceae: *Allium*

Allium cristophii
In cultivation in the UK
Dist: C Anatolia, N, E and C Iran
J F M A **M** J J A S O N D

Allium shelkovnikovii
Nr. Asalem, NW Iran
Dist: NW Iran
J F M A **M** J J A S O N D

Allium bodeanum
From Khorasan, E Iran
Dist: N and E Iran (Gorgan and Khorasan)
J F M A **M** J J A S O N D

Allium derderianum
Kuh-e-Sabelan, N Iran
Dist: N and C Iran
J F M A **M** J J A S O N D

Alliaceae: *Allium*

Allium nigrum
Island of Rhodes
Dist: Turkey-in-Europe, W and S Anatolia, Islands
J F M **A M** J J A S O N D

Allium cardiostemon
Muradiye, E Anatolia
Dist: E Anatolia, NW Iran
J F M A M **J J** A S O N D

Allium orientale
Nr. Eğridir, C Anatolia
Dist: S and C Anatolia
J F M **A M** J J A S O N D

Allium kharputense
Nr. Ovacik, Içel, S Anatolia
Dist: E and S Anatolia, NW Iran
J F M A M **J** J A S O N D

Alliaceae: *Allium/Nectaroscordum*

Allium hirtifolium
Nr. Mariyan, NW Iran
Dist: SE Anatolia, W, C and S Iran

Allium noëanum
Nr. Schulabad, W Iran
Dist: SE Anatolia, W and C Iran

Nectaroscordum

This genus is closely related to *Allium* and two species are found in Turkey and two in Iran; they have distinctive, bell-shaped flowers.

Nectaroscordum siculum (Fig. 149)

The form of this species in Turkey is **ssp. bulgaricum**. The other form, *ssp. siculum*, is found in the western Mediterranean. The *ssp. bulgaricum* has a tall, leafless, 1m stem with 10-30, bell-shaped, greenish-white flowers. It is found rarely in NW Turkey and S Anatolia in fields and on dry, stony hillsides.

The second species, *N. tripedale*, is again rare and comes from E and SE Anatolia and W Iran. It has more numerous white flowers, which are sometimes spotted with pinkish-purple. *N. koelzii* also grows in W Iran and has white flowers.

Nectaroscordum siculum ssp. bulgaricum
Termessos, S Anatolia
Dist: NW Turkey, S Anatolia

Hyacinthaceae

Apart from *Liliaceae* itself species in *Hyacinthaceae* are the most colourful and well-known in the gardening world.

In addition to the usual six stamens and superior ovary, all the members of this family have scaly bulbs and only basal leaves. They have spikes or racemes of relatively small flowers and angular or rounded blackish seeds. The family includes *Urginea*, *Dipcadi*, *Scilla*, *Ornithogalum*, *Puschkinia*, *Hyacinthus*, *Hyacinthella*, *Alrawia*, *Muscari* and *Bellevalia*.

Hyacinthaceae: *Urginea/Dipcadi*

Urginea

This is another genus with only one species in the area.

Urginea maritima (Figs. 150, 151)

This tall plant (up to 1.5m) is a coastal Mediterranean species which is found in W and S Anatolia and the Islands. It has a very large bulb, which is often visible at the soil surface, and the long spike of white flowers appears at the end of summer, often before the autumn rains. It also grows in coastal situations in S Iran.

Urginea maritima
Island of Lesbos
Dist: W and S Anatolia, Islands, S Iran
J F M A M J J A **S O N** D

Urginea maritima
Island of Lesbos
Dist: W and S Anatolia, Islands, S Iran
J F M A M J J A **S O N** D

Dipcadi

Two species of *Dipcadi* are found in Iran, *D. unicolor* in the west and south, and *D. susianum* in the west. *D. unicolor* has racemes of 4-6 pendulous, green flowers, and *D. susianum* has 8-12 greenish-yellow, more erect flowers. One species occurs in W Europe, **D. serotinus**, and this is illustrated **(Fig. 152, 153)** to give an impression of the genus.

Dipcadi serotinus
S Portugal
Dist: Not in our area
J F M **A M J** J A S O N D

Dipcadi serotinus
S Portugal
Dist: Not in our area
J F M **A M J** J A S O N D

Scilla

This genus is very familiar to gardeners with several species commonly grown.

Flowers without bracts

Scilla bifolia (Figs. 154, 155)

This widespread *Scilla* has two, relatively broad leaves and a single spike of up to 20 bright blue flowers. The tepals spread out and give the flowers a starry appearance. It is found in grassy and rocky places close to melting snow, and occurs in Turkey-in-Europe, Outer and S Anatolia and the Islands.

Scilla autumnalis (Figs. 156, 157)

This is the only autumn-flowering species, and has 1 or 2 spikes of 4-25 small, starry, lilac flowers. The many narrow leaves appear after the flowers. The plant grows in macchie and open woods in Turkey-in-Europe, Outer Anatolia and the Islands.

Flowers with bracts. Large plants with many flowers

Scilla hyacinthoides (Fig. 158)

This is a large plant (up to 1m tall) with a single spike of 60-100 flowers. It has 4-8 long, narrow leaves, and the starry, violet-blue flowers have paler margins. It grows in damp meadows and on grassy hillsides in W, S and E Anatolia and the Islands.

Scilla persica (Fig. 159)

This is another large species with 1-3 stems (up to 50cm) of 20-50 starry, blue flowers. It grows in mountain water meadows in SE Anatolia and NW and W Iran.

Flowers with bracts. Smaller plants with leaves as long as the flower spike

Scilla bithynica (not illustrated)

This *Scilla* has 2-3 stems which are 10-30cm tall bearing 3-15 pale blue flowers. The flower spike is conical in shape with the stems of the lower flowers longer than the flower itself. It grows in water meadows and semi-shady, grassy places in the west part of N Anatolia.

Scilla cilicica (Fig. 160)

This species has 2-4 lax spikes of 4-6 pale blue flowers. The 4-6 leaves are quite broad (10-20mm), and the plant is found in woods on limestone in the Cilician Taurus Mountains and also in Cyprus.

Scilla sp. (Fig. 161)

This species is 15-20cm tall and has an upright stem bearing 4-8 open blue flowers. The strap-shaped leaves are of similar length to the scape. It grows in damp mountain grassland near melting snow on Olang Mountain in N Iran. It is most similar in appearance to *S. cilicica* but may be *Scilla siberica ssp. caucasica*.

Scilla hohenackeri (Fig. 162)

The next two species are woodland plants from the Caspian woodlands of N Iran. *Scilla hohenackeri* has 3-6 deep green leaves, and 1-2 stems with 2-7 widely spaced, pale violet-blue flowers. They are pendent and have reflexed tepals.

Scilla greilhuberi (Fig. 163)

This is a similar species to the last with 1-2, 20cm stems of 5-12 blue-violet flowers, which are also pendent and have reflexed tepals.

Scilla melaina (Fig. 164)

This is a species from S Anatolia with 1-3 stems (10-25cm) of 2-3 dull blue, cup-shaped flowers, which grows in sub-alpine meadows and woods.

Scilla monanthos (Fig. 165)

This is another small *Scilla* with 1-2 stems up to 20cm tall, with 1-2 pale blue or whitish flowers with a dark midrib. It is another species of woods and sub-alpine meadows but only grows in NE Anatolia.

Scilla siberica ssp. armena (Fig. 166)

This is another species from NE Anatolia but it grows high in the mountains near melting snow. It has 1-3, 5cm stems bearing 1-2 deep blue, cup-shaped flowers which have a darker midrib and are often white in the centre.

Scilla mischtschenkoana (*S. tubergeniana*) (Fig. 167)

This species from NW Iran has 2-8, 10cm stems bearing 2-6, white or very pale blue, saucer-shaped flowers with a darker midrib. It has 3-4 bright green, relatively broad leaves, and grows in mountain meadows and rocky places.

Flowers with bracts. Smaller plants with leaves distinctly shorter than the flower spike

Scilla rosenii (Fig. 168)

This very attractive species comes from NE Anatolia and has 1-4, 10-15cm stems with 1-2 pale blue flowers with a darker midrib and strongly reflexed tepals. It grows in wet places, often by streams.

Scilla winogradowii (Fig. 169)

This is closely-related species with 1-5, taller (10-30cm) stems and 1-5, lax, pale blue flowers with

Hyacinthaceae: *Scilla*

a darker midrib. It is found in mountain meadows close to melting snow in NE Anatolia.

Scilla gorganica (Fig. 170)
This is a similar species to S *winowgradowii* from Iran. It has 1-4 stems up to 30cm tall bearing a loose inflorescence of 5-10 flowers, which are pendent, grey-blue in colour and have reflexed tepals. It grows in deciduous woodland in the NE region of Iran.

Scilla ingridae (Fig. 171)
This *Scilla* has 2-5 stems, 10-20cm tall bearing 1-3 pale blue-violet flowers, and it grows in mountain meadows and scree, often near melting snow, in S Anatolia.

Scilla leepii (Fig. 172)
This is another small *Scilla* with 1-4 slender stems which are usually single flowered. The flowers are starry in shape and lilac-blue in colour with a dark midrib, and the plant grows in dry steppe in the Upper Euphrates and Mesopotamia regions of E Anatolia.

Other species present in the area include *Scilla mesopotamica* from S Anatolia, *S. khorassanica* from E Iran and *S. bisotunensis* from W Iran.

Scilla bifolia
Nr. Akseki, S Anatolia
Dist: Turkey-in-Europe, Outer and S Anatolia, Islands
J **F M A M J** J A S O N D

Scilla bifolia
Dedegöl Dağ, C Anatolia
Dist: Turkey-in-Europe, Outer and S Anatolia, Islands
J **F M A M J** J A S O N D

Scilla autumnalis
Island of Rhodes
Dist: Turkey-in-Europe, Islands
J F M A M J J **A S O N** D

Hyacinthaceae: *Scilla*

Scilla autumnalis
Guernsey
Dist: Turkey-in-Europe, Islands
J F M A M J J **A S O** N D

Scilla hyacinthoides
Nr. Gaziantep, S Anatolia
Dist: W, S and E Anatolia, Islands
J F M **A M** J J A S O N D

Scilla persica
Baykan, SE Anatolia
Dist: SE Anatolia, NW and W Iran
J F M **A M** J J A S O N D

Scilla cilicica
N Cyprus
Dist: S Anatolia (Cilician Taurus)
J F **M A M** J J A S O N D

Hyacinthaceae: *Scilla*

Scilla sp.
Olang Mountain, N Iran
Dist: N Iran
J F **M A** M J J A S O N D

Scilla hohenackeri
Alborz Mts., N Iran
Dist: N Iran
J F M **A** M J J A S O N D

Scilla greilhuberi
Alborz Mts., N Iran
Dist: N Iran
J F **M A** M J J A S O N D

Scilla melaina
Püren Pass, S Anatolia
Dist: S Anatolia
J F **M A M** J J A S O N D

Hyacinthaceae: *Scilla*

Scilla monanthos
Nr. Artvin, NE Anatolia
Dist: NE Anatolia
J **F M A** M J J A S O N D

Scilla siberica ssp. armena
Kose Dağ, NE Anatolia
Dist: NE Anatolia
J F M **A M** J J A S O N D

Scilla mischtschenkoana
In cultivation in the UK
Dist: NW Iran
J F **M A M** J J A S O N D

Scilla rosenii
Çam Pass, NE Anatolia
Dist: NE Anatolia
J F M A M **J** J A S O N D

Hyacinthaceae: *Scilla*

Scilla winogradowii
Nr. Ardahan, NE Anatolia
Dist: NE Anatolia
J F M **A M** J J A S O N D

Scilla gorganica
Golestan, NE Iran
Dist: N Iran
J F M **A** M J J A S O N D

Scilla ingridae
Aladağlar, S Anatolia
Dist: S Anatolia
J F **M A M J** J A S O N D

Scilla leepii
In cultivation in the UK
Dist: E Anatolia
J F M **A** M J J A S O N D

Hyacinthaceae: *Chionodoxa*

Chionodoxa

Five species of *Chionodoxa* are currently recognised in Turkey. *C. siehei* is frequently grown in gardens, often under the incorrect name of *C. forbesii*, and this has caused much confusion. In the wild many species are very localised and hence distinct. They flower early in the year, often close to melting snow. *Chionodoxa* is distinguished from *Scilla* by having tepals which are fused into a short tube at the base.

Stems 1-2 flowered

Chionodoxa luciliae (*C. gigantea* hort.) (Figs. 173, 174)
This species has 1-2 large, lavender flowers with a diffuse white centre and, unlike other species, the flowers face upwards. It grows on stony, open mountain slopes in the Boz Dağ area of Lydia in W Anatolia.

Stems 4-12 flowered

Chionodoxa forbesii (Fig. 175)
The bright blue flowers of this species are slightly nodding, and they have a distinct, white-coloured central zone. It is much more widely distributed in W and S Anatolia, and grows on open mountain slopes and in coniferous woodland.

Chionodoxa sardensis (Fig. 176)
This multi-flowered species also has flowers that are bright blue, but without the central white zone. It grows at low levels on damp, mossy, north-facing hill slopes in the Izmir area of W Anatolia.

Chionodoxa siehei (Fig. 177, 178)
This species is the one most commonly grown in gardens. The medium-sized flowers face outwards, and they are violet-blue with a large central white eye. It grows on mountain slopes in W Anatolia.

Chionodoxa tmoli (not illustrated)
This species is generally similar to *C. siehei*, but the white zone in the centre of the flowers is so large that only the tips of the tepals are blue. It has broader leaves than other species (up to 3.5cm) and is found in the Tmolus area of W Anatolia.

Chionodoxa luciliae
Boz Dağ, W Anatolia
Dist: W Anatolia (Lydia)
J F M A **M J** J A S O N D

Chionodoxa luciliae
In cultivation at RBG, Kew
Dist: W Anatolia (Lydia)
J F M A **M J** J A S O N D

Hyacinthaceae: *Chionodoxa*

Chionodoxa forbesii
Baba Dağ, SW Anatolia
Dist: W and S Anatolia
J F **M A** M J J A S O N D

Chionodoxa sardensis
In cultivation in Germany
Dist: W Anatolia (Izmir)
J F **M A** M J J A S O N D

Chionodoxa siehei
In cultivation at RBG, Kew
Dist: W Anatolia
J F **M A** M J J A S O N D

Chionodoxa siehei
In cultivation at RBG, Kew
Dist: W Anatolia
J F **M A** M J J A S O N D

Hyacinthaceae: *Puschkinia*

Puschkinia

There is only one species of *Puschkinia* recognised in the Flora of Turkey, *P. scilloides*. However there is at least one additional species and possibly two, but they appear to be unnamed at present. These plants occur high in the mountains and appear as the snow melts.

Puschkinia scilloides (Figs. 179,180)
This widely cultivated species comes from SE Anatolia and N and NW Iran. It is about 20cm tall and has a spike of 2-10 starry, pale blue flowers with a darker blue central line on the tepals. The flower has a central white cone (the corona), formed from the flattened filaments of the stamens, and is 2-3mm long. The plants grow in damp, grassy places in the mountains close to melting snow.

Puschkinia sp. (Fig. 181)
This species is close to the normal *P. scilloides* as it has a similar corona, but the flowers are very small and never open very widely. The leaves are very erect and tend to enclose the flower stem. It grows in lava hollows in the Nemrut Dağ crater on the north side of Lake Van in SE Anatolia. The habitat is drier than normally expected for *P. scilloides*. The form of the flowers and the upright leaves are very similar to the green-flowered species illustrated in The Bulb Book by Phillips and Rix (2nd edition 1989, p. 43).

Puschkinia sp. (Figs. 182,183)
This species grows with *P. scilloides* on the Karabet Pass in SE Anatolia, but is quite distinct. The flowers are on shorter stems and the heads are crowded and rather conical in shape. The white or very pale blue flowers open as soon as they come out of the ground, and they have a small, pale central stripe, but the most distinctive feature is the corona, which is very short or non-existent. The broad leaves tend to spread rather than being upright.

Puschkinia scilloides
Tendürek Pass, E Anatolia
Dist: E and SE Anatolia

Hyacinthaceae: *Puschkinia*

Puschkinia scilloides
Tendürek Pass, E Anatolia
Dist: E and SE Anatolia
J F M **A M J** J A S O N D

Puschkinia sp.
Nemrut Dağ Crater, Lake Van, SE Anatolia
Dist: SE Anatolia
J F M A **M J** J A S O N D

Puschkinia sp.
Karabet Pass, SE Anatolia
Dist: SE Anatolia
J F M A **M J** J A S O N D

Puschkinia sp.
Karabet Pass, SE Anatolia
Dist: SE Anatolia
J F M A **M J** J A S O N D

Ornithogalum

The *Ornithogalum* genus (Star of Bethlehems) is a difficult one in this area as there are many species of similar appearance. In Turkey there are about 25 species and in Iran about 12 species, 7 of which are also found in Turkey. The shape, length, number and hairiness of the leaves are important characteristics, as are stem length, and form of the spike or umbel in fruit.

The genus can be divided into four main groups:

A. Relatively tall plants with a generally cylindrical inflorescence. Filaments unwinged. Ovary green.

B. Relatively short or stemless plants with a more umbel-like inflorescence. This group represents the bulk of the species.

C. Plants with a cylindrical inflorescence. Filaments winged. Ovary green. (*O. nutans* only)

D. Tall plants with a cylindrical or umbel-like inflorescence that is many-flowered. Ovary black and very obvious.

Group A

Ornithogalum pyrenaicum (Fig. 184)
This is the only species to have greenish-yellow, rather than white, flowers. It is up to 1m tall and the flowers are small, about 25-40 in number, with narrow tepals. It occurs in grassland in NW Turkey, NE, Inner and SW Anatolia and the Islands.

Ornithogalum sphaerocarpum (Fig. 185)
This species is very similar to *O. pyrenaicum* but has 15-25 small, white flowers in a shorter inflorescence. It is widespread in Anatolia and occurs in a broad range of habitats.

Ornithogalum narbonense (Fig. 186)
This species is widespread in the Mediterranean region. It has a narrow, cylindrical inflorescence up to 60cm tall with 25-75 white flowers. As with most *Ornithogalum* species the tepals are white on the inside and have a strong green stripe on the outside. The pedicels (flower stalks) are erect in fruit. It grows on stony slopes and fields, is widespread in Anatolia, and has occasionally been reported from Iran.

Ornithogalum shelkovnikovii (Fig. 187)
This is a similar, but rather shorter, species from E Anatolia. It is rather glaucous in appearance and the linear leaves are u-shaped in cross-section. It has fewer flowers (10-25) and a rather broader inflorescence, with pedicels that are divergent in fruit. It occurs in stony fields and sub-alpine meadows, often in wet places.

Ornithogalum arcuatum (Fig. 188)
This *Ornithogalum* is also similar to *O. narbonense* but it is an altogether larger and more robust plant. It can be over 1m in height and has many flowers in a rather broad, cylindrical inflorescence. The pedicels curve upwards in fruit. It is another species found in grassy places in E Anatolia, and also in N and NW Iran.

Ornithogalum bungei (Fig. 189)
This is a very distinctive species from NE Iran, where it grows in deciduous woodland. It has a long stem (60cm) with a narrow, congested spike of short-pedicelled flowers.

Group B

Plants with leaves which have ciliate margins and are hairy on the underside

Ornithogalum armeniacum (Fig. 190)
With this species the stem is evident (up to 20cm) and the leaves are long and narrow exceeding the flower scape. There are 7-11 flowers which are white with the typical green stripe on the outside. The fruiting pedicels are spreading. It is common on stony slopes and meadows in W and S Anatolia and the Islands.

Ornithogalum fimbriatum (Fig. 191)
This is a very similar species to *O. armeniacum* with a very short stem and 4-8 flowers. However the fruiting pedicels are sharply deflexed and are somewhat thickened at the base. It is found in NW Turkey and the Islands.

Plants with leaves which have ciliate margins and are glabrous on the underside

Ornithogalum ulophyllum (Fig. 195)
This is a species with a distinct stem 7-25cm in height, and rather broader leaves (7-9mm), which are distinctively undulate and often red-margined. The fruiting pedicels are held stiffly at an angle of 45°. It is found on calcareous slopes and in macchie throughout Anatolia except in the east.

Ornithogalum comosum (not illustrated)
This species is similar to *O. ulophyllum* but without undulate leaves.

Hyacinthaceae: *Ornithogalum*

Plants with leaves that are glabrous on all surfaces

Leaves broad and flat, usually held close to the ground

Ornithogalum lanceolatum (Fig. 192)
This species has a very short stem and many long leaves that are 1.5-2cm broad. The tight corymb of 5-13 large flowers is found in forests, and on slopes and steppe in S Anatolia.

Ornithogalum montanum (Fig. 196)
This species has a distinct stem (10-20cm) and several 8-15mm wide leaves that are shorter than the scape. The rather open flower head has 7-14 flowers and the pedicels are spread widely in fruit. It grows on hillsides and in meadows in W Turkey, S Anatolia and the Islands.

Leaves quite broad but held erect

Ornithogalum oligophyllum (Fig. 193, 194)
This species is distinguished by the 2-3 channelled leaves which exceed the flowers, are narrow at the base, but broaden out and end abruptly in a rounded, hooded apex. The flower stem is about 15cm and bears 2-5 flowers, and the fruiting pedicels are erect. It is a mountain species found on rocky slopes, often near snow patches, and occurs throughout Anatolia except for the west, and in NW Iran.

Ornithogalum wiedemanniae (Fig. 197)
This species is similar to *O. oligophyllum* but is distinguished by its winged fruit. The linear leaves exceed the flowers and the fruiting pedicels are spreading. It grows on shady hillsides in widely scattered localities.

Ornithogalum platyphyllum (not illustrated)
This is a species with quite a tall stem (15-30cm) and several erect leaves which are 10-15mm wide at ground level and taper gradually to an acute apex. It has 6-15 flowers and the fruiting pedicels are erect. It is found in marshy places in Inner Anatolia.

Leaves long and narrow exceeding the scape. Flowering stem very short or non-existent

Ornithogalum sigmoideum (Figs. 198, 199)
This species has numerous narrow, channelled leaves and few (3-6) flowers. It has a delicate appearance and the green band on the outside of the tepals is faint. The fruiting pedicels are sharply deflexed into the ground, and the plant is found in pinewoods and shady places in N and S Anatolia and in N Iran.

Ornithogalum sintenisii (Fig. 200)
This is a similar species which is endemic to N Iran, with again long, channelled leaves and few flowers. It is another woodland species, particularly deciduous woodland, and has spreading pedicels in fruit.

Ornithogalum alpigenum (Fig. 201)
This Turkish endemic species has a short flowering stem and several long, erect leaves with a white line on the upper surface. It has 4-7 flowers and spreading fruiting pedicels. It is often found in large clumps on hills and steppe in SW and S Anatolia.

Ornithogalum orthophyllum (Fig. 202)
This species is similar to the last with again a white line on the upper surface of the long, narrow leaves. The short scape has 10-20 flowers and the fruiting pedicels are spreading. It is widespread in scrub and meadows in Anatolia and N and NW Iran.

Leaves long and narrow exceeding the scape. Flowering stem up to 30cm

Ornithogalum umbellatum (Fig. 203)
This is another clump-forming species and is the most widely distributed *Ornithogalum* in the European area, and in our area it is mainly found in cultivated fields in N Turkey and W and S Anatolia. It has a 10-30cm stem with 6-20 flowers. The leaves are narrow with a white line above and they exceed the flowers. The fruiting pedicels are very long and rigid and they spread horizontally.

Group C

Ornithogalum nutans (Fig. 204)
This is the only member of this group and is distinguished botanically by its winged filaments. However it is distinctly different to any other species and is readily recognised. It grows in fields and meadows in W, C and S Anatolia and the Islands.

Group D

Ornithogalum persicum (Fig. 205)
This is a relatively tall plant with a dense, cylindrical, many-flowered spike with flowers with an obvious black ovary. The 6-8 leaves are 20-30mm broad and overlap at the base of the stem, but are shorter than the scape. It is found in fallow fields in E Anatolia and NW and W Iran.

Ornithogalum arabicum (Fig. 206)
This is a widespread Mediterranean species with a long stem (up to 80cm) and leaves rather narrower than with *O. persicum*. The flower spike is flat-topped and dense with 6-25 large flowers, and the black ovary is very visible. It is found in rocky places in Turkey-in-Europe and the Islands.

> Other species recorded in Turkey include *O. sorgerae*, *O. pumilum*, *O. refractum*, *O. exaratum*, *O. nivale* and *O. sphaerolobum*, and in Iran *O. brachystachys*, *O. pycnanthum* and *O. cuspidatum*.

Hyacinthaceae: *Ornithogalum*

Ornithogalum pyrenaicum
Bath, England
Dist: NW Turkey, NE to SW Anatolia, Islands
J F M A **M J** J A S O N D

Ornithogalum sphaerocarpum
Maraş, S Anatolia
Dist: Widespread except S Anatolia
J F M **A M J** J A S O N D

Ornithogalum narbonense
Nr. Bireçik, S Anatolia
Dist: Widespread
J F M **A M J** J A S O N D

Ornithogalum shelkovnikovii
Muradiye, E Anatolia
Dist: E Anatolia
J F M A **M J** J A S O N D

Hyacinthaceae: *Ornithogalum*

Fig 188

Ornithogalum arcuatum
Lake Van, SE Anatolia
Dist: E Anatolia, N and NW Iran
J F M A M **J J A** S O N D

Fig 189

Ornithogalum bungei
Golestan, NE Iran
Dist: NE Iran
J F M **A M** J J A S O N D

Fig 190

Ornithogalum armeniacum
Nr. Eğridir, S Anatolia
Dist: W and S Anatolia, Islands
J F M **A M J J A** S O N D

Hyacinthaceae: *Ornithogalum*

Ornithogalum fimbriatum
Island of Chios
Dist: NW Turkey and Islands
J F M A M J J A S O N D

Ornithogalum lanceolatum
Nr. Adana, S Anatolia
Dist: S Anatolia
J F M A M J J A S O N D

Ornithogalum oligophyllum
Güzeldere Pass, SE Anatolia
Dist: NE and E Anatolia
J F M A M J J A S O N D

Hyacinthaceae: *Ornithogalum*

Ornithogalum oligophyllum
Karabet Pass, SE Anatolia
Dist: NE and E Anatolia
J F **M A M J** J A S O N D

Ornithogalum ulophyllum
Nr. Eğridir, S Anatolia
Dist: Anatolia except the east
J F **M A M J** J A S O N D

Ornithogalum montanum
Tekir, Maraş, S Anatolia
Dist: W Turkey, S Anatolia and the Islands
J F **M A M** J J A S O N D

Ornithogalum wiedemannii
Püren Pass, Maraş, S Anatolia
Dist: Widespread in Anatolia
J F **M A M J** J A S O N D

Hyacinthaceae: *Ornithogalum*

Ornithogalum sigmoideum
Amanus Mts., S Anatolia
Dist: N and S Anatolia, N Iran
J F **M A M J** J A S O N D

Ornithogalum sigmoideum
Nr. Chelgerd, W Iran
Dist: N and S Anatolia, N Iran
J F **M A M J** J A S O N D

Ornithogalum sintenisii
Golestan, NE Iran
Dist: N Iran
J F M **A M** J J A S O N D

Hyacinthaceae: *Ornithogalum*

Ornithogalum alpigenum
Ahir Dağ, Maraş, S Anatolia
Dist: SW and S Anatolia
J F M **A M J J** A S O N D

Fig 201

Fig 202

Ornithogalum orthophyllum
Sisakht, W Iran
Dist: Widespread in Anatolia, N and NW Iran
J F **M A M** J J A S O N D

Ornithogalum umbellatum
Nr. Antalya, S Anatolia
Dist: N Turkey, W and S Anatolia, Islands
J F **M A M** J J A S O N D

Fig 203

Hyacinthaceae: *Ornithogalum*

Ornithogalum nutans
Nr. Eğridir, S Anatolia
Dist: W, C and S Anatolia, Islands
J F **M A M** J J A S O N D

Fig 204

Fig 205

Ornithogalum persicum
Kermanshah, W Iran
Dist: E Anatolia, NW and W Iran
J F M A **M J** J A S O N D

Ornithogalum arabicum
Island of Chios
Dist: Turkey-in-Europe, Islands
J F M **A M J** J A S O N D

Fig 206

Hyacinthaceae: *Muscari*

Muscari

The familiar 'grape hyacinths', represented by the blue-flowered, dense-headed *Muscari* species, are known to all gardeners, but the extent of the genus, and the less common Muscarinia and Leopoldia sections of the group, are less well known.

All species have only basal leaves and a raceme of separated fertile and sterile flowers. The 6 stamens are attached about halfway up the tubular corolla of the small flowers, which are often constricted at the mouth. The outer lobes of the corolla (the teeth) are often a contrasting colour to the main bell.

Except for *M. parviflorum* they are all spring-flowering.

Muscarimia Section

Muscari muscarimi (Figs. 207, 208)

This distinctive species has a lax spike of ivory, cream or grey-green flowers with prominent teeth, which start the same colour as the rest of the flower but later turn brown. It comes from SW and S Anatolia where it grows on scree and steppe slopes. Both this and the next species are strongly scented.

Muscari macrocarpum (Figs. 209, 210)

This is the only *Muscari* with bright yellow flowers, and these are similar in form to those of *M. muscarimi* but are rather larger in size, so it is a spectacular plant. As its name suggests it has very large seed-pods (2.5 by 3.5cm). It grows in SW Anatolia and the Islands in macchie on stony slopes, often near the sea.

Leopoldia Section

Muscari comosum (Figs. 211, 212)

The so-called 'tassel hyacinth' is the first member of another distinctive group. Most have brownish, widely-spaced, fertile flowers, and small purple sterile flowers at the top of the spike. *Muscari comosum* is the largest of these with a stem of up to 80cm and up to 100 flowers. Its distinctive feature is that the pedicels (flower stems) of the purple or violet sterile flowers are much longer than those of the pale brown fertile flowers.

This species is common in the general Mediterranean region, and is widespread in Anatolia (except the north) and the Islands, and in W and SW Iran. It grows in open woodland, on rocky slopes and in fallow fields.

Muscari weissii (Fig. 213)

This is a similar but smaller plant up to 30cm tall with a lax raceme of brown fertile flowers with bright yellow teeth to the corolla. The blue to purple sterile flowers have pedicels of a similar length to those of the fertile ones. The plant grows on rocky slopes and in phrygana in SW Anatolia and the Islands.

Muscari tenuiflorum (Fig. 214)

This member of the group has a 20-60cm spike of lax, virtually sessile, fertile flowers which are violet in bud, but are pale brown in flower, with brown to blackish, re-curved tips to the corolla. The sterile flowers are bright violet and are again conspicuous. It is widespread on slopes and in steppe in Inner Anatolia, and in Iran.

Muscari caucasicum (Figs. 215, 216)

This species is up to 30cm tall with a lax raceme of up to 150 flowers, the fertile ones having a brownish corolla with yellowish teeth. The deep violet, short pedicelled, sterile flowers form a conspicuous, dense, upright tuft to the flower spike. The plant grows on stony slopes and steppe in Inner Anatolia, and in W, NW and N Iran.

Also in this section are *Muscari longipes* and *M. massayanum*. The former occurs in Inner Anatolia and W Iran, and the latter is a Turkish endemic from S and E Anatolia.

The Botryanthus Group

This is the group that would be generally recognised as 'grape hyacinths', with dense heads of blue to violet flowers.

Muscari aucheri (Figs. 217, 218)

This typical species is not as well known or as widely cultivated as *Muscari armenaicum* or *M. neglectum*. It has 2-3, quite broad leaves which are grey-green and have a hooded apex, and appear with the flowers. The bright blue, fertile flowers have small white teeth, and the few sterile flowers are much paler. It grows on stony slopes and in mountain pastures in Outer and C Anatolia.

Muscari armeniacum (Figs. 219, 220)

This is a common grape hyacinth in cultivation. It has more, narrower leaves than the previous species and these are produced in the autumn. The dense head has many, mid-blue, fertile flowers with small white teeth, and a few, paler, sterile flowers. It is widespread in Anatolia and is often present in large numbers in damp pastures. It also grows on stony slopes and in open woodland and scrub.

Muscari neglectum (Figs. 221,222)

This species is the most common type in cultivation, and in the wild it is widespread in Anatolia and the Islands, and in N and W Iran. It has several narrow leaves which are produced in autumn, and has a dense spike of dark blue to violet, fertile flowers with small white teeth. Again the sterile flowers are paler. It grows in macchie, scrub and meadows, and on rocky slopes.

Muscari commutatum (Figs. 223,224)

This similar species is widespread in the Mediterranean region, but in Turkey it only occurs on the Islands. It has deep violet-blue, fertile flowers with teeth of the same colour. The sterile flowers are similar but have a paler pedicel. It grows in phrygana, olive groves and on grassy terraces.

Muscari latifolium (Fig. 225)

This species is distinguished by its single, broad leaf, and its dense spike of deep violet, fertile flowers with pale lilac teeth. The sterile flowers are also pale lilac. The plant is found in coniferous forests in W and S Anatolia.

Muscari bourgaei (Fig. 226)

This small *Muscari* has 3-6 linear leaves and a rather lax spike of bright blue, fertile flowers with white or pale blue teeth. The sterile flowers are usually the same colour. It is a mountain species occurring in mountain meadows and on stony slopes in NW, W and S Anatolia.

Muscari anatolicum (Figs. 227,228)

This small *Muscari* is distinguished by the very prominent white teeth of the corolla of the deep blackish-blue, fertile flowers. The sterile flowers are a brighter blue. Pink-flowered forms are occasionally found (**Fig. 228**). The 5-10 linear leaves do not have the paler median line of many of the species in this group. It grows on rocky slopes in Inner and S Anatolia.

Muscari sandrasicum (Fig. 229)

This is a very small-flowered species with a short spike of blue or violet fertile flowers with very small, white teeth. The sterile flowers are often absent, but if a few are present they are of similar colour. It grows in high mountain pastures and screes in SW Anatolia.

Other species in this group include *Muscari microstomum* and *M. adilii*.

The Pseudomuscari Group

Plants in this group have fertile flowers that are open at the mouth rather than being constricted, and they have very few sterile flowers. All are spring-flowering other than the autumn-flowering *M. parviflorum*.

Muscari inconstrictum (Fig. 230)

This species is typical of the group with very dark blue, fertile flowers with teeth of the same colour and an open mouth. It grows in phrygana in the Amanus Mountains of S Anatolia, and in NW Iran.

Muscari azureum (Figs. 231,232)

The leaves of this species appear with the flowers and it has a short, dense spike of sky-blue, fertile flowers and a few, paler sterile flowers. The lobes of the flowers are a similar colour to the rest of the corolla, which has a central, darker stripe. It grows on rocky slopes and in sub-alpine meadows in Anatolia, mostly west of the Anatolian Diagonal.

Muscari macbeathianum (Fig. 233)

This distinctive species has a spike of pale lilac flowers that turn white as they fully open. Sterile flowers are usually absent. *M. macbeathianum* grows in open pine woodland in the Adana area of S Anatolia.

Muscari discolor (Fig. 234)

This small endemic species has dense heads of blackish-blue, fertile flowers, with or without a few paler sterile flowers. There is a whitish band near the white, re-curved teeth of the corolla. It grows in steppe at about 1,000m in the Mesopotamian area of S Anatolia

Muscari pseudomuscari (*M. chalusicum*) (Figs. 235,236)

This is another species with sky-blue flowers, and in the wild it comes from shady cliffs in the Chalus Valley and the Alborz Mountains of N Iran. The 3-4 leaves appear well before the flowers, which have a darker stripe down the corolla, as with *M. azureum*. Sterile flowers are few if any.

Muscari coeleste (Fig. 237)

This endemic *Muscari* comes from alpine slopes and pastures, often near melting snow, in E Anatolia. The rather lax spike of sky-blue flowers is about 10cm tall, and the 2-3 leaves are channelled and taper to a point.

Muscari parviflorum (Fig. 238)

This is distinctive as it is the only autumn-flowering species. The flowers are small and often few (7-12) and the colour is pale to sky-blue, with whitish outer lobes. The sterile flowers are very small or absent. It grows on rocky slopes and in olive groves and orchards near the coast in Outer Anatolia and the Islands.

Hyacinthaceae: *Muscari*

Muscari muscarimi
Nr. Manavgat, S Anatolia
Dist: S and SW Anatolia
J F **M A M J** J A S O N D

Muscari muscarimi
In cultivation in Turkey
Dist: S and SW Anatolia
J F **M A M J** J A S O N D

Muscari macrocarpum
In cultivation in the UK
Dist: SW Anatolia, Islands
J **F M A** M J J A S O N D

Muscari macrocarpum
Marmaris, SW Anatolia
Dist: SW Anatolia, Islands
J **F M A M** J J A S O N D

Hyacinthaceae: *Muscari*

Muscari comosum
Nr. Manavgat, S Anatolia
Dist: Widespread in Anatolia, Islands, W and SW Iran
J F **M A M** J J A S O N D

Muscari comosum
Island of Rhodes
Dist: Widespread in Anatolia, Islands, W and SW Iran
J F **M A M** J J A S O N D

Muscari weissii
Island of Rhodes
Dist: SW Anatolia, Islands
J F **M A M** J J A S O N D

Muscari tenuiflorum
From Kop Dağ, E Anatolia
Dist: Widespread in Inner Anatolia, N, W and SW Iran
J F M **A M** J J A S O N D

Hyacinthaceae: *Muscari*

Muscari caucasicum
Muradiye, E Anatolia
Dist: Inner Anatolia, W, NW and N Iran
J F **M A M J** J A S O N D

Muscari caucasicum
Nr. Eğridir, Inner Anatolia
Dist: Inner Anatolia, W, NW and N Iran
J F **M A M J** J A S O N D

Muscari aucheri
Lake Abant, Bolu, NW Anatolia
Dist: Outer and C Anatolia
J F M **A M J** J A S O N D

Muscari aucheri
Davraz Dağ, Eğridir, Inner Anatolia
Dist: Outer and C Anatolia
J F M **A M J** J A S O N D

Hyacinthaceae: *Muscari*

Muscari armeniacum
Nr. Erzurum, E Anatolia
Dist: Widespread in Anatolia
J F **M A M** J J A S O N D

Muscari armeniacum
Nr. Ibradi, S Anatolia
Dist: Widespread in Anatolia
J F **M A M** J J A S O N D

Muscari neglectum
Nr. Chelgerd, W Iran
Dist: Widespread in Anatolia, Islands, N and W Iran
J F **M A M** J J A S O N D

Muscari neglectum
Island of Rhodes
Dist: Widespread in Anatolia, Islands, N and W Iran
J F **M A M** J J A S O N D

Hyacinthaceae: *Muscari*

Muscari commutatum
Island of Samos
Dist: Islands
J **F M A** M J J A S O N D

Muscari commutatum
Island of Lesbos
Dist: Islands
J **F M A** M J J A S O N D

Muscari latifolium
Nr. Akseki, S Anatolia
Dist: W and S Anatolia
J F M **A M** J J A S O N D

Muscari bourgaei
In cultivation at RBG, Kew
Dist: NW, W and S Anatolia
J F M A **M J** J A S O N D

Hyacinthaceae: *Muscari*

Muscari anatolicum
Nr. Ibradi, SAnatolia
Dist: Inner and S Anatolia
J F M **A M J** J A S O N D

Muscari anatolicum *(pink form)*
Nr. Ibradi, SAnatolia
Dist: Inner and S Anatolia
J F M **A M J** J A S O N D

Muscari sandrasicum
From Sandras Dağ, Özhatay, SW Anatolia
Dist: SW Anatolia
J F M A M **J J** A S O N D

Muscari inconstrictum
Ma'Loula, Syria
Dist: S Anatolia (Amanus), NW Iran
J F **M** A M J J A S O N D

Hyacinthaceae: *Muscari*

Muscari azureum
Nr. Gülek, S Anatolia
Dist: Scattered in Anatolia
J F **M A M** J J A S O N D

Muscari azureum
Tekir Dağ, S Anatolia
Dist: Scattered in Anatolia
J F **M A M** J J A S O N D

Muscari macbeathianum
In cultivation in the UK
Dist: S Anatolia (Adana)
J F **M A M** J J A S O N D

Muscari discolor
From Gaziantep, S Anatolia
Dist: S Anatolia (Mesopotamia)
J F **M A M** J J A S O N D

Hyacinthaceae: *Muscari*

Muscari pseudomuscari
From Mazandaran, N Iran
Dist: N Iran
J F M **A** M J J A S O N D

Muscari pseudomuscari
In cultivation at RBG, Kew
Dist: N Iran
J F M **A** M J J A S O N D

Muscari coeleste
Kop Dağ, E Anatolia
Dist: E Anatolia
J F M **A M** J J A S O N D

Muscari parviflorum
Nr. Ovaçik, Içel, SW Anatolia
Dist: Outer Anatolia, Islands
J F M A M J J **A S O N** D

Hyacinthaceae: *Hyacinthus*

Hyacinthus

The Turkish species of *Hyacinthus*, *H. orientalis*, is the source of all the cultivated hyacinths. It is the only species to occur in Turkey, but two other species, *H. litwinowii* and *H. transcaspicus*, grow in Iran.

Hyacinthus orientalis (Figs. 239–241)

Two subspecies are present in Turkey, **ssp. orientalis**, on limestone slopes at lower levels (up to 1,500m) in S Anatolia, and **ssp. chionophilus** at higher levels on rocky slopes and scree, often near melting snow, in central south Anatolia.

The former has leaves that are 4-5mm wide and often grows in clumps, whereas the latter has much broader leaves (12-15mm) and is often solitary. The *ssp. chionophilus* has a stem that is strongly spotted at the base, and both forms have spikes of large, grey-blue or violet-blue flowers.

Hyacinthus litwinowii (Figs. 242,243)

This species has 3-5 broad, glaucous leaves and one or two, 10-20cm stems of 3-10 pale blue flowers. It grows in damp, shady places amongst scrub at altitudes of 1,500-2,000m in N Iran.

Hyacinthus transcaspicus (not illustrated)

Hyacinthus transcaspicus has 2-6 narrower leaves and a single, 5-10cm spike of deeper blue flowers. It is another Iranian mountain species, which flowers in May and June, often near melting snow, and grows in the eastern Alborz Mountains and in northern Khorasan.

Fig 239

Hyacinthus orientalis ssp. chionophilus
Püren Pass, Maraş, S Anatolia
Dist: Central S Anatolia
J F M A **M J** J A S O N D

Fig 240

Hyacinthus orientalis ssp. orientalis
Nr. Ibradi, S Anatolia
Dist: S Anatolia
J F **M A** M J J A S O N D

Hyacinthaceae: *Hyacinthus*

Hyacinthus orientalis ssp. orientalis
Nr. Ibradi, S Anatolia
Dist: S Anatolia
J F **M A** M J J A S O N D

Fig 241

Fig 242

Hyacinthus litwinowii
Golestan, N Iran
Dist: N Iran
J F **M A** M J J A S O N D

Hyacinthus litwinowii
Golestan, N Iran
Dist: N Iran
J F **M A** M J J A S O N D

Fig 243

Hyacinthaceae: *Bellevalia*

Bellevalia

The *Bellevalia* genus is very close to *Muscari* and there are species resembling the typical grape hyacinths, such as *B. forniculata* and *B. pycnantha*, and species similar to the tassel hyacinths, such as *B. dubia* and *B. longistyla*. A significant botanical difference between the two genera is that with *Bellevalia* the stamens are attached at the base of the corolla rather than halfway up.

Inflorescence lax and cylindrical. Leaves not ciliate.

Bellevalia trifoliata (Fig. 244)
The three broad leaves of this species are longer than the 30cm flower spike, which has 20-40 flowers that are violet in bud, and whitish with a brown base to the corolla when fully open. It grows in damp meadows and stony places at low altitudes in NW Turkey, W Anatolia and the Islands.

Bellevalia dubia (Fig. 245)
This is a similar species with 2-5 channelled leaves, but the flower buds are blue and the corolla is pale violet with white, green-veined outer lobes. It is found only rarely in grassy places in W Anatolia.

Bellevalia tauri (Fig. 246)
This member of the same group has 3-4 glaucous, linear leaves which are quite wide (up to 18mm). The flower buds are violet and the corolla brownish with pale green lobes. It grows in upland fields in SW and S Anatolia.

Inflorescence lax. Leaves ciliate.

Bellevalia longistyla (Fig. 247)
This species has about five broad green leaves, and a lax, 15-25 flowered raceme. The pedicels of the flowers are long (up to 20mm) and the lowest elongate in fruit to 5-8cm. The flower buds are purplish and the corolla is purple with white, green-veined lobes. It grows on dry hillsides and in steppe in E Anatolia and NW and W Iran.

Bellevalia longipes (Fig. 248)
This is a similar species from steppe habitats in E Anatolia and W Iran. It has 5-6 broad leaves and 1-2 stems up to 45cm tall, and the flowers have pedicels up to 25mm long. In fruit the lower pedicels elongate to up to 15cm, giving the spike a conical shape. The flowers are purplish with green-veined lobes.

Bellevalia gracilis (Fig. 249)
This is a smaller plant with whitish flower buds and a brownish corolla with paler lobes. The fruiting raceme is again conical in shape, but the pedicels are deflexed towards the end of flowering. It grows in fields and on stony hillsides in S and E Anatolia.

Bellevalia kurdistanica (Fig. 250)
This is a very local species from steep slopes in the Hakkari area of SE Anatolia. It has 5-6 leaves which are longer than the 1-2 flower stems. The pedicels are short and the flower buds and corolla are greenish-white, turning violet towards the base.

Inflorescence dense and globular. Leaves not ciliate.

Bellevalia rixii (Fig. 251)
This is a small species from stony slopes and scree at about 3,000m in SE Anatolia. It has 2-3 leaves which are twisted and curved in a sickle shape, and a head of a few purple-brown flowers.

Bellevalia forniculata (Figs. 252–254)
This *Bellevalia* cannot be confused with any other species because of its bright, sky-blue flowers. It grows in wet mountain meadows in NE Anatolia, and, although local, it is often present in large numbers.

Bellevalia pycnantha (Fig. 255)
This and the next species, *B. paradoxa*, are often considered to be the same, but there are certainly very different forms. The form of *B. pycnantha* illustrated here is the many-flowered, very dark violet form from E Anatolia and W Iran. The inner lobes of the corolla have white to pale yellow margins, and the spike becomes more lax as the fruits develop. It generally grows in wet meadows and hillsides.

Bellevalia paradoxa (Fig. 256)
This rather smaller species has a dense spike of 10-18 flowers, which are blue in bud and darken to deep blue-violet, with the corolla lobes the same colour. It grows in alpine pastures at about 2,500m in NE Anatolia.

Bellevalia fominii (Fig. 257)
This species has 3-5 narrower, glaucous leaves and a more lax flower spike, and the corolla is greenish with the inner lobes being blackish at the apex. It grows in mountain meadows in SE Anatolia.

Bellevalia tristis (Fig. 258)
This species, from steppe and stony hillsides in W Iran, also has more lax flower spikes. It has 4-6 channelled, glaucous leaves, and a short raceme of 10-20 reddish-violet flowers with greenish outer lobes.

Many other species of *Bellevalia* are recognised in both Turkey and Iran, but they are difficult to identify and can be very localised in their distribution.

Hyacinthaceae: *Bellevalia*

Bellevalia trifoliata
Island of Rhodes
Dist : NW Turkey, W Anatolia, Islands
J F **M A M** J J A S O N D

Bellevalia dubia
Nr. Izmir, W Anatolia
Dist: W Anatolia (rare)
J F M **A M** J J A S O N D

Bellevalia tauri
Püren Pass, S Anatolia
Dist: SW and S Anatolia
J F **M A M** J J A S O N D

Bellevalia longistyla
Nr. Chelgerd, W Iran
Dist: E Anatolia, W and NW Iran
J F M **A M** J J A S O N D

Hyacinthaceae: *Bellevalia*

Bellevalia longipes
Takht-e Suleyman, W Iran
Dist: E Anatolia, W Iran
J F **M A** M J J A S O N D

Bellevalia gracilis
Ahir Dağ, Maraş, S Anatolia
Dist: S and E Anatolia
J F M A **M J** J A S O N D

Bellevalia kurdistanica
In cultivation in Turkey
Dist: SE Anatolia (rare)
J F M A **M** J J A S O N D

Bellevalia rixii
Nr. Van, SE Anatolia
Dist: SE Anatolia
J F M A **M** J J A S O N D

Hyacinthaceae: *Bellevalia*

Bellevalia forniculata
Nr. Erzurum, E Anatolia
Dist: NE Anatolia
J F M A **M J** J A S O N D

Bellevalia forniculata
Nr. Erzurum, E Anatolia
Dist: NE Anatolia
J F M A **M J** J A S O N D

Bellevalia forniculata
Nr. Ardahan, NE Anatolia
Dist: NE Anatolia
J F M A **M J** J A S O N D

Hyacinthaceae: *Bellevalia*

Bellevalia pycnantha
Nr. Chelgerd, W Iran
Dist: E Anatolia, W Iran
J F M A **M J** J A S O N D

Bellevalia paradoxa
Karabet Pass, SE Anatolia
Dist: E Anatolia
J F M A M **J** J A S O N D

Bellevalia fominii
Karabet Pass, SE Anatolia
Dist: SE Anatolia, NW Iran
J F M A **M J** J A S O N D

Bellevalia tristis
Semirom, W Iran
Dist: W Iran
J F M **A M J** J A S O N D

Hyacinthaceae: *Hyacinthella*/*Alrawia*

Hyacinthella

This is a group of small, broad-leaved bulbous species with blue or violet flowers. The number of leaves and the presence or absence of flower pedicels are characteristic.

Flowers sessile (without stems) or with short stems

Hyacinthella heldreichii (Figs. 259, 260)
This species has the typical pair of leaves with the first relatively broad and the second narrower. The 5-15cm stem elongates in fruit, and bears 10-15 dark violet flowers. The flowers are usually sessile or short pedicelled, but can sometimes have longer pedicels (Fig. 260). It grows in scrub, in open pine forests and on stony hillsides in S. and C. Anatolia.

Hyacinthella nervosa (Fig. 261)
This species has two broader leaves and a rather dense, 10-25 flowered raceme of sessile, blue to pale blue flowers. It grows on open calcareous slopes and steppe in the Mesopotamian region of S Anatolia.

Flowers with distinct stems

Hyacinthella hispida (Fig. 262)
This species also has two leaves, but both are covered with long hairs. The base of the 10cm stem is purple-spotted and bears a rather lax raceme of 10-20 dark violet flowers. It grows in oak scrub and scree in S. Anatolia.

Hyacinthella glabrescens (Fig. 263)
This species is similar to *H. heldreichii*, but the leaves are rather broader and the short-pedicelled flowers are more blue-violet. It grows on dry stony slopes and scree in the Cilician Taurus area of S. Anatolia.

Hyacinthella acutiloba (Fig. 264)
This species has three leaves with the first up to 15mm broad and the others narrower. The 10cm flower stem is often purple-spotted and the 6-25 flowered raceme is rather lax. The flowers are deep blue in colour and white forms sometimes occur. It grows in oak scrub and on bare, stony slopes in C. Anatolia.

Four other endemic species of *Hyacinthella* are found in Turkey, and an additional species in Iran (*H. persica*).

Alrawia

Alrawia is a genus closely related to *Hyacinthella* and there are two species in Iran, *A. nutans* and *A. bellii*. They are broad-leaved, purple-flowered plants with larger, longer pedicelled flowers than typical *Hyacinthella* species. Both occur in W. Iran.

Fig 259
Hyacinthella heldreichii
Nr. Akseki, S. Anatolia
Dist: S and C Anatolia
J **F M A M** J J A S O N D

Fig 260
Hyacinthella heldreichii
Nr. Akseki, S Anatolia
Dist: S and C Anatolia
J **F M A M** J J A S O N D

Hyacinthaceae: *Hyacinthella*

Fig 261

Hyacinthella nervosa
Nr. Gaziantep, S Anatolia
Dist: S Anatolia (Mesopotamia)
J F **M A** M J J A S O N D

Fig 262

Hyacinthella hispida
In cultivation in Turkey
Dist: S Anatolia (Içel, Adana)
J **F M A** M J J A S O N D

Fig 263

Hyacinthella glabrescens
In cultivation in the UK
Dist: S Anatolia (Cilician Taurus)
J F **M A** M J J A S O N D

Fig 264

Hyacinthella acutiloba
In cultivation in the UK
Dist: C Anatolia
J F M **A M** J J A S O N D

Liliaceae

The relevant genera retained within *Liliaceae* are *Lilium*, *Fritillaria*, *Tulipa*, *Erythronium* and *Gagea*, so this family contains some of the most spectacular and well-known bulbous plants. All are bulbous perennials and many produce fruiting capsules with numerous flat brown seeds.

As with most monocotyledons the parts of the flower are arranged in two groups of three, the outer three being the equivalent of sepals in other plants, and the inner three equivalent to the petals. However in this family both groups are similar or identical, and this leads to the term 'tepals' for all six parts.

One other term arises in this family, particularly in *Fritillaria*, and that is 'tessellated'. This describes the spotted appearance of the tepals in these genera, *Fritillaria meleagris* being a typical example.

Liliaceae: *Lilium*

Lilium

Although there are many lily species worldwide, in our area there are only eight, seven in Turkey and one in Iran. In Turkey most species are concentrated in N and NE Anatolia, particularly in the mountains along the Black Sea coast.

Lilium candidum (Fig. 265)
This very well known, white-flowered lily grows in macchie and deciduous forest in SW Anatolia and the Islands. It is up to 1.2m tall and occurs at relatively low levels.

Lilium martagon (Fig. 266)
This is another widely distributed and familiar lily which is found in NW Turkey. The pink, purple-spotted flowers are on stems 1m tall and it grows in shady places, usually in deciduous woodland.

Lilium carniolicum ssp. ponticum (*Lilium ponticum*) (Figs. 267, 268)
This is one of the widespread lilies in NE Anatolia and occurs in both yellow and orange-flowered forms. It is rather shorter in stature than the previous species and grows in mountain meadows and shady places above the tree line.

Lilium ciliatum (Figs. 269, 270)
This is another Pontic lily which is up to 1.5m tall. It has 2-10 cream-coloured flowers with a brown centre, and the leaves have ciliate margins. It grows in open places in woodland or mountain meadows on acid soils.

Lilium monadelphum (Figs. 271, 272)
This is another tall lily with 1-5 large, pale-yellow flowers. Two varieties are recognised, *v. szovitsianum* and *v. armenum*, but differences between them are small, mainly depending on the width of the tepals. It occurs in NE Anatolia in open forests and meadows at lower levels, below the tree line.

Lilium kesselringianum (Figs. 273, 274)
This is probably the largest of the lily species in the area with 1-7 large, strongly scented, cream-coloured flowers. It grows on wooded slopes and in meadows at about 2,000m in NE Anatolia.

Lilium akkusianum (Fig. 275)
This species was only named in 1996 when it was found in the Akkus area of N Anatolia. This is further west than the areas where most of the lily species are found. *Lilium akkusianum* has up to 25 white to pale-yellow flowers with orange-red anthers, on a stem up to 1.8m tall. It grows in open places in deciduous woodland.

Lilium ledebourii (Fig. 276)
This is the only lily species in Iran, where it grows in the Mazandaran area in woods near the Caspian Sea. It is tall (up to 1.5m) and has 2-15 white flowers.

Liliaceae: *Lilium*

Lilium candidum
Muğla, SW Anatolia
Dist: SW Anatolia, Islands
J F M A **M J** J A S O N D

Lilium martagon
Bolu, NW Turkey
Dist: NW Turkey
J F M A M **J J** A S O N D

Lilium carniolicum ssp. ponticum
Ovit Dağ, NE Anatolia
Dist: NE Anatolia
J F M A **M J** J A S O N D

Lilium carniolicum ssp. ponticum
Ovit Dağ, NE Anatolia
Dist: NE Anatolia
J F M A **M J** J A S O N D

Liliaceae: *Lilium*

Lilium ciliatum
Uzundere, Giresun, NE Anatolia
NE Anatolia
J F M A M **J J** A S O N D

Lilium ciliatum
Uzundere, Giresun, NE Anatolia
NE Anatolia
J F M A M **J J** A S O N D

Lilium monadelphum
Zigana Pass, Trabzon, NE Anatolia
Dist: NE Anatolia
J F M A M **J J** A S O N D

Lilium monadelphum
Zigana Pass, Trabzon, NE Anatolia
Dist: NE Anatolia
J F M A M **J J** A S O N D

Liliaceae: *Lilium*

Lilium kesselringianum
Çam Pass, NE Anatolia
Dist: NE Anatolia
J F M A M **J J** A S O N D

Lilium kesselringianum
Çam Pass, NE Anatolia
Dist: NE Anatolia
J F M A M **J J** A S O N D

Lilium akkusianum
S of Akkus, Ordu, N Anatolia
Dist: Akkus Area, N Anatolia
J F M A M **J J** A S O N D

Lilium ledebourii
From Mazandaran, N Iran
Dist: N Iran
J F M A M **J J** A S O N D

Liliaceae: *Fritillaria*

Fritillaria gibbosa, Golestan, NE Iran

Liliaceae: *Fritillaria*

Fritillaria

Many species in this genus are very distinctive and easily recognised from the photographs, and they do not need a detailed description here. This section therefore concentrates on some of the more difficult groups which can be very confusing, particularly when they grow together in similar habitats.

The inner three petals of a fritillary each have a well-developed nectary at the base and this can be important in terms of identification. Equally the form of the style and stigma are important diagnostic features.

Fritillaria imperialis (Figs. 278–280)
The stately Crown Imperial is well known to gardeners, but it is a magnificent sight in its wild setting in W Iran. It grows in large numbers on clayey hillsides near Chelgerd and Aligudarz in the Zagros Mountains of western Iran, and in a few places in SE Anatolia. In the wild it is nearly always orange in colour.

Fritillaria raddeana (Figs. 281, 282)
This yellow-green flowered fritillary is another tall plant and it is found in damp places at the base of hills in NE Iran.

Fritillaria gibbosa (Figs. 277, 283)
This distinctive fritillary is up to 30cm tall and grows in very dry, stony places on hills in N and W Iran. It is widely distributed and sometimes occurs in large numbers.

Fritillaria ariana (Fig. 284)
This pink-flowered species is closely related to *F. gibbosa*, but is rare and localised in Iran, occurring only close to the Afghan border east of Mashad.

Fritillaria persica (Figs. 285–288)
This is an easily recognised fritillary but in the wild it is quite variable. In western Iran the forms normally found have relatively few greenish or yellowish flowers, whereas those found in southern Anatolia are more brown or purplish in colour and are taller with many flowers. In particular the purple-brown form from the Adiyaman area (Fig. 288) is popular in cultivation.

Fritillaria latifolia (Figs. 289, 290)
This short-stemmed, tubby-flowered fritillary is found on high passes on stony ground or in mountain meadows in NE Anatolia. Its purple flowers are tessellated and rather square in shape.

Fritillaria aurea (Fig. 291)
This is another distinctive species which has a similar flower shape to *F. latifolia*. It is also tessellated, but yellow in colour, and is found amongst rocks and snow patches on limestone in C and S Anatolia.

Fritillaria pontica (Fig. 292)
This green-flowered fritillary has its centre of distribution in the Balkans, and is only found in our area in open woods in N Turkey and on some of the Islands. It is quite tall (up to 45cm) with larger flowers than most of the green-flowered species, and has 8 narrow leaves, the upper three in a whorl. The nectaries are circular and blackish.

Fritillaria acmopetala (Fig. 293)
This fritillary is readily recognised by the reddish-brown markings at the base of the inner tepals and their yellow edging. It also has a large flower and there are two subspecies recognised **ssp. acmopetala** which is taller (up to 45cm) with seven narrow leaves and a round-shouldered bell, and **ssp. wendelboi** with four broader leaves and an angular-shouldered bell. The *ssp. acmopetala* is found in open woods in SW and S Anatolia and *ssp. wendelboi* in cedar forest at higher levels in S Anatolia only.

Fritillaria whittallii (Fig. 294)
This species resembles our native *F. meleagris* but is rather darker in colour with strong brown tessellations. It is a forest species found in rocky places amongst conifers in S and SW Anatolia.

Fritillaria reuteri (Figs. 295, 296)
This attractive fritillary is unusual in that it is found in very wet places, often at the edge of streams, in W Iran.

Fritillaria amana (Fig. 297)
This species is about 30cm tall with 1-2 green flowers which have inner tepals tessellated or purple at the edges. It occurs in shady, rocky places, mainly in the Amanus Mountains of S Anatolia. In some forms it resembles *Fritillaria crassifolia ssp. crassifolia* but differences in the nectaries distinguish them.

Fritillaria straussii (Figs. 298, 299)
This fritillary is about 30cm tall and has 1-2 flowers which are green when they are fresh, but tend to darken to reddish-brown. They are tessellated all over and are found amongst oak scrub in SE Anatolia and W Iran.

Fritillaria michailovskyi (Fig. 300)
This is another fritillary that is well known and widely cultivated. In the wild it is endemic to a small area of E Anatolia, where it grows at between 2,000 and 3,000m on open stony hillsides. It has up to 5 brown, yellow-edged flowers on a short stem.

Fritillaria crassifolia
This small, but variable, fritillary has three subspecies, **ssp. crassifolia** (Fig. 301), **ssp. kurdica** (Figs.

302–304) and **ssp. hakkarensis** (Fig. 305). The three subspecies are distinguished by the leaves, the flower colour and the nectaries. *Ssp. crassifolia* normally has four alternate leaves which are quite broad and glaucous, and the nectary does not have a raised ridge. The other subspecies both have 5-7 leaves which are longer and narrower, and a nectary with a raised ridge. The leaves of *ssp. kurdica* are glaucous and those of *ssp. hakkarensis* are shining green. *Ssp. crassifolia* occurs on very loose scree in scattered places in NE and S Anatolia, and the other subspecies are found in SE Anatolia. The latter two sometimes grow together, *ssp. kurdica* on open stony hillsides or screes and *ssp. hakkarensis* in snow patch hollows. *Ssp. kurdica* also occurs in NW Iran. As can be seen from the photographs, *ssp. kurdica* is very variable and in some forms **(Fig. 304)** it can resemble *F. michailovskyi*, but the green line down the centre of the tepals in the former distinguishes them. A new form of *F. crassifolia* that probably deserves ssp. status has recently been found in the Kordestan area of W Iran **(Fig. 306)**. It has red-brown flowers with a strong yellow tip to the tepals or all-yellow flowers.

Fritillaria kotschyana (Figs. 307, 308)
This is a large-flowered species from N and NW Iran. It has two forms, **ssp. kotschyana** with green flowers that are tessellated on the outer and inner surfaces, and **ssp. grandiflora** with dark purple, tessellated flowers. The *ssp. kotschyana* occurs at high levels (2,000-3,000m) on rocky slopes and screes in NW Iran, and *ssp. grandiflora* grows at somewhat lower levels in rocky places and open woodland in N Iran.

Fritillaria olivieri (Fig. 309)
This species is endemic to W Iran where it occurs in damp places by streams. It is up to 30cm tall and has green and brown flowers without tessellations.

Fritillaria alfredae (Fig. 310)
This is another green-flowered species with two forms recognised in Turkey, **ssp. platyptera** with seven narrow leaves and long bract leaves, and **ssp. glaucoviridis** with 9-11 broader leaves and shorter bract leaves. Both grow in oak scrub in S Anatolia, the former having a rather more easterly distribution in this area.

Fritillaria minuta (Figs. 311, 312)
This is a very distinctive small-flowered species with open, toffee-coloured flowers and rather broad, bright green leaves. It grows in the mountains by late snow patches in E and SE Anatolia.

Fritillaria alburyana (Figs. 313, 314)
This is one of the most distinctive fritillaries and needs no description, but it has recently been found in NE Anatolia growing with *F. armena*, and the spectacular natural hybrid shown in **(Fig. 315)** was growing nearby. This has the general flower size and shape of *F. armena* but the pink colour of *F. alburyana*.

Fritillaria sororum (Fig. 316)
This is a recently named species, which has been found in the Gulnar region of S Anatolia. It has narrow, channelled leaves and purplish-brown flowers which are tessellated inside and out.

Fritillaria fleischeriana (Fig. 317)
This short fritillary (up to 15cm) has 1-3 purplish-brown flowers, with a green stripe on the tepals and yellow edging. It grows in stony steppe and scrub in W and C Anatolia.

Fritillaria bithynica (Fig. 318)
This a small green-flowered fritillary with a quite different distribution, growing mainly in NW and W Anatolia and the Islands. The 1-2 flowers are glaucous to yellowish-green and the plant is found in oak scrub and low level pine forests.

Fritillaria viridiflora (not illustrated)
This is a small, green-flowered fritillary found rarely in S Anatolia in stony fields which are flooded in winter. It is similar to *F. bithynica* but larger.

Fritillaria stribrnyi (Fig. 319)
This rare species, recorded from Turkey-in-Europe, can be tall (60cm) and has 1-3, glaucous, green, purple-edged flowers. It is another species closely related to *F. bithynica*.

Fritillaria rhodia (Fig. 320)
This yellow-green flowered fritillary is only found on the island of Rhodes, where it occurs at the edge of pinewoods and in open, stony ground. It is quite tall (30cm) and has 10-14 narrow green leaves.

A very similar but smaller species, **F. pelinea (Fig. 321)**, occurs on the island of Chios around Mount Pelineon.

Fritillaria sibthorpiana (Fig. 322)
The next few species are all yellow-flowered. The first, *F. sibthorpiana*, is closely related to *F. carica*. It has 2-3 oval leaves and the solitary flowers are bell-shaped with a very stout style. It is found in pine forests on limestone in SW Anatolia.

Fritillaria forbesii (Fig. 323)
This species has 1-2 narrow, bell-shaped, greenish-yellow flowers and 5-10 linear leaves. It occurs in pine forests or macchie on serpentine soils in SW Anatolia.

Fritillaria carica (Figs. 324, 325)
This is another fritillary with two subspecies in Turkey. The first, **ssp. carica**, has 6-7 leaves and narrow, bell-shaped flowers, and comes from limestone soils in W Anatolia and the Islands. The other, **ssp.**

serpenticola, has 4-5 leaves and larger, broader, conical flowers and occurs on serpentine soils in SW Anatolia.

Fritillaria minima (Figs. 326,327)
The final species in this group is *F. minima* and this has a totally different distribution, being found on high passes near melting snow in SE Anatolia.

Fritillaria caucasica (Fig. 328)
The next group, consisting of *F. caucasica*, *F. armena*, *F. pinardii* and *F. assyriaca* is very confusing as they are generally similar and often grow together and probably hybridise in E Anatolia. They all have purplish-brown flowers and glaucous leaves.

F. caucasica has solitary, rounded, bell-shaped flowers which are dark purplish brown with a glaucous bloom, and the slender, entire style is often exserted. It is found in damp alpine pastures on peaty soils in N and NE Anatolia and NW Iran.

Fritillaria armena (Fig. 329)
This species has 4-5 leaves and 1-3 flowers which are dark purplish brown inside and out, again with a purplish bloom on the outside. The style divides into three at the outer end. It is found at high levels in the mountains of E Anatolia, usually by late snow patches.

Fritillaria pinardii (Figs. 330,331)
This is a widely distributed and variable fritillary occuring in N, Inner and S Anatolia and NW and W Iran. It is shorter than the previous species (up to 20cm) and its 1-2 bell-shaped flowers are purplish to greyish outside, usually with a small yellow tip, and yellow inside. The style is variable and can be slender or stout and divided into three or undivided. The plant is often found near late snow patches.

Fritillaria zagrica (Figs. 332,333)
This species is closely related to *F. pinardii* and is mainly found in NW and W Iran, but it has been reported also from SE Anatolia. Unlike *F. pinardii* the cylinder-shaped flowers are very constant, with a dark, purplish-brown outside and a distinct yellow tip.

Fritillaria assyriaca (Fig. 334)
This species has 1-2 narrow, greenish or purplish-brown flowers and 4-6 narrow glaucous leaves with hooded tips. The style is club-shaped. The plant can be quite tall (30cm) and is found in mountain steppe or cultivated fields in E Anatolia.

A form from S Anatolia, **ssp.melananthera** (Fig. 335) has a more striped bell, rather like *F. chlororhabdota*.

Fritillaria chlororhabdota (Fig. 336)
There is some confusion as to whether *F. assyriaca* occurs in Iran. The illustrated species is thought to be *F. chlororhabdota* but it may be more correctly described as *F. assyriaca ssp. iranica*. It grows in the Zagros mountains in western Iran and is clearly related to *F. assyriaca*, but the purplish-grey, green-lined flowers, with their open bell-shape, are quite distinct.

Fritillaria kittaniae (Fig. 337)
This fritillary is related to *F. pinardii* and has solitary flowers which are pale purple in colour with a broad green stripe on the outside of the outer tepals. The inner tepals are yellow. It grows in cedar forests in the Taurus Mountains of S Anatolia.

Fritillaria elwesii (Fig. 338)
This is another species that is similar to *F. assyriaca* but it comes from low level macchie in S Anatolia. Like *F. chlororhabdota* it has brownish-purple flowers with a strong green stripe. The style is stout and 3-branched.

Fritillaria latakiensis (Fig. 339)
This fritillary has 1-2 narrow, bell-shaped flowers which are purplish outside and greenish-yellow inside. It is found in SW and S Anatolia at low levels in deciduous scrub.

Fritillaria uva-vulpis (Fig. 340)
This species, from damp meadows in SE Anatolia and NW Iran, has 1-2 rounded, bell-shaped flowers which are brownish-grey outside and yellowish inside. The style is short and undivided.

Liliaceae: *Fritillaria*

Fritillaria imperialis
Clayey and rocky slopes near Chelgerd, W Iran
Dist: NW and W Iran and SE Anatolia
J F **M A M J** J A S O N D

Fig 278

Fritillaria imperialis
Clayey and rocky slopes near Chelgerd, W Iran
Dist: NW and W Iran and SE Anatolia
J F **M A M J** J A S O N D

Fig 279

Fritillaria imperialis
Clayey and rocky slopes near Chelgerd, W Iran
Dist: NW and W Iran and SE Anatolia
J F **M A M J** J A S O N D

Fig 280

Liliaceae: *Fritillaria*

Fritillaria raddeana
Damp places at the base of hills, Golestan, NE Iran
Dist: NE Iran

Fritillaria raddeana
Damp places at the base of hills, Golestan, NE Iran
Dist: NE Iran

Fritillaria gibbosa
Very dry, stony ground, Golestan, NE Iran
Dist: N and W Iran

Fritillaria ariana
In cultivation in Germany
Dist: NE Iran

Liliaceae: *Fritillaria*

Fritillaria persica
Nr. Gulnar, S Anatolia
Dist: NW and W Iran and S Anatolia
J F M **A M** J J A S O N D

Fritillaria persica
Clayey slopes near Chelgerd, W Iran
Dist: NW and W Iran and S Anatolia
J F M **A M** J J A S O N D

Fritillaria persica
Rocky slopes near Mersin, S Anatolia
Dist: NW and W Iran and S Anatolia
J F M **A M** J J A S O N D

Fritillaria persica (Adiyaman form)
In cultivation in the UK
Dist: NW and W Iran and S Anatolia
J F M **A M** J J A S O N D

Liliaceae: *Fritillaria*

Fritillaria latifolia
Alpine meadows, Çam Pass, NE Anatolia
Dist: NE Anatolia
J F M A **M J J** A S O N D

Fritillaria latifolia
Stony ground, Kose Dağ, NE Anatolia
Dist: NE Anatolia
J F M A **M J J** A S O N D

Fritillaria aurea
Nr. Malatya, S Anatolia
Dist: C and S Anatolia
J F M A **M J J** A S O N D

Fritillaria pontica
Ulu Dağ, Bursa, N Turkey
Dist: N Turkey and Islands
J F M **A M** J J A S O N D

Liliaceae: *Fritillaria*

Fig 293

Fritillaria acmopetala ssp. acmopetala
Nr. Eğridir, S Anatolia
Dist: SW and S Anatolia
J F M **A M J** J A S O N D

Fig 294

Fritillaria whittallii
Kaznak Forest, Eğridir, S Anatolia
Dist: S and SW Anatolia
J F M **A M J** J A S O N D

Fig 295

Fritillaria reuteri
Wet places at the edge of streams, near Chelgerd, W Iran
Dist: W Iran
J F M **A M J** J A S O N D

Fig 296

Fritillaria reuteri
Wet places at the edge of streams, near Chelgerd, W Iran
Dist: W Iran
J F M **A M J** J A S O N D

Liliaceae: *Fritillaria*

Fritillaria amana
Püren Pass, Maraş, S Anatolia
Dist: S Anatolia
J F M **A M** J J A S O N D

Fritillaria straussii
Shady, stony places, Karun Valley, W Iran
Dist: SE Anatolia and W Iran
J F M **A M** J J A S O N D

Fritillaria straussii
In cultivation in the UK
Dist: SE Anatolia and W Iran
J F M **A M** J J A S O N D

Fritillaria michailovskyi
Stony hillsides, Tahir Pass, E Anatolia
Dist: E Anatolia
J F M A **M** J J A S O N D

Liliaceae: *Fritillaria*

Fritillaria crassifolia* ssp. *crassifolia
Mt. Palandoken, Erzurum, E Anatolia
Dist: NE and S Anatolia
J F M A **M J** J A S O N D

Fritillaria crassifolia* ssp. *kurdica
Güzeldere Pass, SE Anatolia
Dist: SE Anatolia and NW and W Iran
J F M **A M J** J A S O N D

Fritillaria crassifolia* ssp. *kurdica
Güzeldere Pass, SE Anatolia
Dist: SE Anatolia and NW and W Iran
J F M **A M J** J A S O N D

Fritillaria crassifolia* ssp. *kurdica
Tendürek Pass, E Anatolia
Dist: SE Anatolia and NW and W Iran
J F M **A M J** J A S O N D

Liliaceae: *Fritillaria*

Fig 305

Fritillaria crassifolia* ssp. *hakkarensis
Semdinli, SE Anatolia
Dist: SE Anatolia
J F M A **M J J** A S O N D

Fig 306

Fritillaria crassifolia (Iran form)
Kordestan, W Iran
Dist: W Iran
J F M **A M** J J A S O N D

Fig 307

Fritillaria kotschyana* ssp. *kotschyana
Kandovan Pass, NW Iran
Dist: NW Iran
J F M **A M J J** A S O N D

Fig 308

Fritillaria kotschyana* ssp. *grandiflora
Deciduous woods, Olang, N Iran
Dist: N Iran
J F M **A M** J J A S O N D

129

Liliaceae: *Fritillaria*

Fritillaria olivieri
In cultivation in the UK
Dist: W Iran
J F M A M J J A S O N D

Fritillaria alfredae ssp glaucoviridis
In cultivation in the UK
Dist: S Anatolia
J F M A M J J A S O N D

Fritillaria minuta
Nemrut Dağ crater, SE Anatolia
Dist: E and SE Anatolia and NW Iran
J F M A M J J A S O N D

Fritillaria minuta
Nemrut Dağ crater, SE Anatolia
Dist: E and SE Anatolia and NW Iran
J F M A M J J A S O N D

Liliaceae: *Fritillaria*

Fritillaria alburyana
Kop Dağ, E Anatolia
Dist: E Anatolia
J F M A **M J J** A S O N D

Fritillaria alburyana
Kop Dağ, E Anatolia
Dist: E Anatolia
J F M A **M J J** A S O N D

Fritillaria alburyana* x *F. armena
E Anatolia

Liliaceae: *Fritillaria*

Fritillaria sororum
Gulnar, S Anatolia
Dist: S Anatolia
J F **M A** M J J A S O N D

Fritillaria fleischeriana
From Eskişehir, C Anatolia
Dist: W and C Anatolia
J **F M A M** J J A S O N D

Fritillaria bithynica
Çanakkale, W Anatolia
Dist: NW and W Anatolia, Islands
J F **M A M** J J A S O N D

Fritillaria stribrnyi
In cultivation in the UK
Dist: Turkey-in-Europe
J F M **A M** J J A S O N D

Liliaceae: *Fritillaria*

Fritillaria rhodia
Nr. Lindos, Island of Rhodes
Dist: Island of Rhodes
J F **M A** M J J A S O N D

Fritillaria pelinea
Mount Pelineon, Island of Chios
Dist: Island of Chios
J F **M A** M J J A S O N D

Fritillaria sibthorpiana
In cultivation in the UK
Dist: SW Anatolia
J F **M A** M J J A S O N D

Fritillaria forbesii
Baba Dağ, SW Anatolia
Dist: SW Anatolia
J **F M** A M J J A S O N D

Liliaceae: *Fritillaria*

Fritillaria carica* ssp. *carica
From Muğla, SW Anatolia
Dist: W Anatolia, Islands
J F **M A M** J J A S O N D

Fritillaria carica* ssp. *serpenticola
In cultivation in Turkey
Dist: SW Anatolia
J F M **A M** J J A S O N D

Fritillaria minima
Karabet Pass, SE Anatolia
Dist: SE Anatolia
J F M A **M J J** A S O N D

Fritillaria minima
Karabet Pass, SE Anatolia
Dist: SE Anatolia
J F M A **M J J** A S O N D

Liliaceae: *Fritillaria*

Fritillaria caucasica
Tendürek Pass, NE Anatolia
Dist: N and NE Anatolia
J F M **A M** J J A S O N D

Fritillaria armena
Çat Pass, E Anatolia
Dist: E Anatolia
J F M **A M** J J A S O N D

Fritillaria pinardii
Muğla, SW Anatolia
Dist: N, Inner and S Anatolia and NW and W Iran
J F M **A M** J J A S O N D

Fritillaria pinardii
Ahir Dağ, Maraş, S Anatolia
Dist: N, Inner and S Anatolia and NW and W Iran
J F M **A M** J J A S O N D

135

Liliaceae: *Fritillaria*

Fig 332

Fritillaria zagrica
Nr. Khomeyn, W Iran
Dist: NW, C and W Iran and SE Anatolia
J F **M A M** J J A S O N D

Fig 333

Fritillaria zagrica
Nr. Chelgerd, W Iran
Dist: NW, C and W Iran and SE Anatolia
J F **M A M** J J A S O N D

Fig 334

Fritillaria assyriaca
Tendürek Pass, NE Anatolia
Dist: E Anatolia
J F **M A M** J J A S O N D

Fig 335

Fritillaria assyriaca ssp. melananthera
Silifke, S Anatolia
Dist: S Anatolia
J F **M A M** J J A S O N D

Fig 336

Fritillaria chlororhabdota
Nr. Chelgerd, W Iran
Dist: W Iran
J F M **A M** J J A S O N D

Liliaceae: *Fritillaria*

Fritillaria kittaniae
From Sinekçibeli Pass, S Anatolia
Dist: S Anatolia (Antalya)
J F M **A** M J J A S O N D

Fritillaria elwesii
Nr. Akseki, S Anatolia
Dist: S Anatolia
J F **M A M** J J A S O N D

Fritillaria latakiensis
Nr. Antakya, S Anatolia
Dist: S and SW Anatolia
J F M A **M J** J A S O N D

Fritillaria uva-vulpis
In cultivation in the UK
Dist: SE Anatolia
J F M A **M J** J A S O N D

137

Tulipa

The identification of tulips from western and central Asia has always caused difficulties as there are large numbers of nominally similar species. Botanically tulips are classified into groups on the basis of their bulb tunic and characteristics such as presence or absence of hairs on the filaments, but for the sake of simplicity they have been divided here on the basis of flower colour and geographical area.

White or Pink-flowered Tulips

Tulipa biflora (Fig. 341)
Despite its name this tulip has one to three small flowers with white tepals and a yellow centre. It has two narrow glaucous leaves and is found high in the mountains of E Anatolia and N and W Iran.

A very closely related species **T. polychroma** (Fig. 342) is found in W and NW Iran.

Tulipa humilis (Figs. 345–348)
This is another small-flowered species but the flower is very variable in colour, from white through pink to purple, with a yellow blotch at the base of the tepals. The pink form is probably the most widespread and occurs in S and SE Anatolia and N and NW Iran.

Tulipa violacea var. *pallida* (Fig. 349)
This tulip from central Iran is almost certainly a form of *T. humilis*. It has white flowers with a blue blotch at the tepal base, and is found very locally.

Tulipa saxatilis (Fig. 350)
This is a pink-flowered tulip with broad, glossy green leaves which is found in rocky places in SW Anatolia.

Tulipa clusiana (Figs. 351,352)
This very distinctive species has white flowers with a black central blotch, and the three outer tepals have a strong pink stripe on the outer surface. It is a native of W Iran, but is naturalised in W Turkey and some of the islands.

Yellow-flowered Tulips

Tulipa sylvestris (Fig. 343)
This single-flowered tulip is widespread in the Mediterranean region, and in our area it is found in W and S Anatolia and N and NW Iran. It often grows in cultivated fields, but can also be found high in the mountains.

Tulipa biebersteiniana (Fig. 344)
This is closely related to *T. sylvestris* and is very similar in appearance, but it can have several flowers on a stem. It grows in woodland in N Iran.

Tulipa urumiensis (Fig. 377)
This tulip has only been found on the northern shores of Lake Urmiah in NW Iran. It is in cultivation, but has not been seen in the wild in recent times.

Tulipa montana (Figs. 373,374)
This tulip is usually bright red, but yellow forms occur, often growing together with the normal form. It is endemic to N Iran and grows on stony hillsides. The small blotch at the base of the tepals is light brown. The yellow-flowered forms are often called v. *chrysantha*.

Tulipa mucronata (Fig. 378)
This is a yellow form of *T. armena* from N Iran. As can be seen in the figure it is often taller than the Turkish forms of this species.

Red-flowered Tulips in Turkey

These can be divided between the relatively low-level, coastal and field tulips such as *T. orphanidea*, *T. praecox* and *T. agenensis*, and those growing in stony places in the mountains, such as *T. armena* and *T. julia*. *T. undulatifolia* and *T. sintenisii* occur in a variety of habitats.

Tulipa agenensis (Figs. 358,359)
This species occurs in W Turkey and the islands, and can be identified from the unequal bright red tepals, the outer three being longer than the inner. The flowers have large black basal blotches with a strong yellow margin. It is a tall tulip most often found in cultivated ground.

Tulipa praecox (Fig. 360)
This tulip is found in similar places to *T. agenensis*, but is dull, pinky-red in colour. It does not open very widely and has a brownish blotch with yellow edging.

Tulipa orphanidea (Figs. 353,354)
This is orange-red, or occasionally yellow, in colour with a dark blotch and a yellowish stripe on the outside of the outer tepals, and it is restricted to stony fields in W Turkey.

A closely related species, **T. whittallii** (Fig. 355), is found in the Çanakkale area.

Liliaceae: *Tulipa*

Tulipa armena (Figs. 356,357)
There are two subspecies of this tulip in Turkey, **ssp. armena** and **ssp. lycica**. They are similar in appearance having relatively small, short-stalked, red flowers, with a small black blotch, and they are distinguished by differences in the bulb tunic. However *ssp. armena* is mainly found in NE Anatolia (and in NW Iran), and *ssp. lycica* is found in S and C areas. This species sometimes has a yellow line down the centre of the tepals.

Tulipa julia (Fig. 361)
Predominantly found in E Anatolia *T. julia* is a mountain tulip, usually of short stature. It is orange-red in colour with the usual black, yellow-margined blotch. The outer tepals are usually pinkish or yellowish at the base. It is occasionally found in a yellow form.

Tulipa sintenisii (Figs. 364,379)
This species is found in central and E Anatolia in cultivated land or on stony hillsides. The flowers are larger than *T. armena* and are usually distinctly yellow in bud **(Fig. 363)**. Once again the inside of the tepals have a black blotch with a small yellow margin. The stems are short and the leaves are somewhat undulating and glaucous.

Tulipa undulatifolia (Fig. 362)
As the name suggests this tulip has strongly undulate leaves which are quite narrow and glaucous. It occurs in coastal habitats in W Turkey and at higher levels in central Anatolia.

Tulipa sprengeri (Fig. 365)
This late-flowering tulip is widely cultivated but for many years was thought to be extinct in the wild. It was originally found in the Amasya area of N Anatolia and has apparently been recently re-found in the wild. The flower is orange-red in colour and has a very distinctive shape.

Other Species in Turkey
Also illustrated **(*Tulipa sp.*, Fig. 366)** is a red and yellow striped tulip occuring to the west of Erzurum. This population is all this colour and has three or four glaucous leaves. The habitat is a stony hillside above the road. It is probably the species that has been described as *T. kaghyzmanica*.

Species present in Turkey but not illustrated include *T. aleppensis* from S Turkey, and the recently-named *T. cinnabarina* from the Taurus mountains.

Red flowered Tulips in Iran

Of the red-flowered species already described *T. armena* and *T. julia* also occur in NW Iran, but many other species are widespread here. They are often growing in very dry, stony, steppe conditions in the mountains of the north and west.

Tulipa micheliana (Fig. 369)
This is one of the easiest tulips to identify as the narrow, glaucous, undulate leaves have purple lines along their length. The short-stemmed flowers are large and bright red with large, black, yellow-edged blotches which show through strongly on the outside of the tepals.

Tulipa systola (*T. stapfii*) (Fig. 368)
This bright-red, large-flowered species grows in open forest and mountain conditions in N and W Iran. The tepals have a large black blotch at the base with quite a narrow yellow margin. The leaves are broad and often green to blue-green in colour.

Tulipa hoogiana (Fig. 370)
This is another large-flowered tulip with very bright, glossy, red flowers, which have black blotches at the base of the tepals with a strong yellow margin. The stem is often short and the glaucous leaves are relatively long. It grows in the steppe zone of NE Iran.

Tulipa ulophylla (Fig. 371)
This tulip is purplish-red in colour and has many narrow glaucous leaves. The black blotch at the base of the tepals has almost no yellow margin and the filaments and anthers are violet. It occurs in the Alborz mountains of N Iran.

Tulipa montana (Fig. 372)
This is one of the most common tulips in N Iran and is often present in large numbers and a variety of colours. The dominant colour is red, but yellow and orange forms occur. The flowers are cup-shaped and only have a small dark blotch. The filaments are red at the top and dark at the base.

Tulipa wilsoniana (Fig. 367)
This is a tall tulip growing in open woodland in NE Iran (Golestan). It has rather small flowers which do not open very widely, and five or six long, narrow stem leaves. It may be a woodland form of *T. montana*.

Tulipa schrenkii (Fig. 375)
This tulip is reported from N Iran and in cultivation it has bright red flowers with an orange-yellow edge to the tepals. In the wild it is apparently more variable in colour, and can be red or yellow.

Tulipa linifolia (Fig. 376)
This widely cultivated, small red tulip has been reported from NE Iran (Golestan). It has six to eight narrow, glaucous leaves and is most commonly found in central Asia.

Species not illustrated but present in Iran are *T. sogdiana*, *T. lehmanniana* and *T. kuschkensis*.

Liliaceae: *Tulipa*

Tulipa biflora
Golestan, N Iran
Dist: S and SE Anatolia, N and NW Iran
J F **A M** J J A S O N D

Tulipa polychroma
Nr Semirom, W Iran
Dist: W and NW Iran
J F **A M** J J A S O N D

Tulipa sylvestris
Mountain slopes, Davraz Dağ, Inner Anatolia
Dist: W and C Anatolia, W and NW Iran
J F **A M** J J A S O N D

Tulipa biebersteiniana
Golestan, N Iran
Dist: N Iran
J F **A M** J J A S O N D

Liliaceae: *Tulipa*

Fig 345

Tulipa humilis
Güzeldere Pass, SE Anatolia
Dist: S and SE Anatolia, W and NW Iran
J F M **A M J** J A S O N D

Fig 346

Tulipa humilis
Güzeldere Pass, SE Anatolia
Dist: S and SE Anatolia, W and NW Iran
J F M **A M J** J A S O N D

Fig 347

Tulipa humilis
Karabet Pass, SE Anatolia
Dist: S and SE Anatolia, W and NW Iran
J F M **A M J** J A S O N D

Fig 348

Tulipa humilis
Chelgerd, W Iran
Dist: S and SE Anatolia, W and NW Iran
J F M **A M J** J A S O N D

Liliaceae: *Tulipa*

Fig 349

Tulipa violacea v. pallida
In cultivation at RBG, Kew
Dist: C Iran
J F **M A** M J J A S O N D

Fig 350

Tulipa saxatilis
Nr. Antalya, S Anatolia
Dist: W and C Anatolia
J F M **A M** J J A S O N D

Fig 351

Tulipa clusiana
Island of Chios
Dist: W Turkey and Islands, W Iran
J F **M A** M J J A S O N D

Fig 352

Tulipa clusiana
Island of Chios
Dist: W Turkey and Islands, W Iran
J F **M A** M J J A S O N D

Liliaceae: *Tulipa*

Tulipa orphanidea
Çanakkale, W Turkey
Dist: W Turkey, Islands
J F **M A M** J J A S O N D

Tulipa orphanidea
Muğla, SW Anatolia
Dist: W Turkey, Islands
J F **M A M** J J A S O N D

Tulipa whittallii
Çannakale, W Turkey
Dist: W Turkey
J F **M A M** J J A S O N D

Tulipa armena ssp. armena
Nr. Erzurum, NE Anatolia
Dist: NE Anatolia, NW Iran
J F M **A M** J J A S O N D

Tulipa armena ssp. lycica
Ahir Dağ, S Anatolia
Dist: S and C Anatolia
J F M **A M** J J A S O N D

143

Liliaceae: *Tulipa*

Tulipa agenensis
Island of Chios
Dist: Outer Anatolia, Islands
J F M **A** M J J A S O N D

Tulipa agenensis
Island of Chios
Dist: Outer Anatolia, Islands
J F M **A** M J J A S O N D

Tulipa praecox
Island of Chios
Dist: W Anatolia, Islands
J F M **A** M J J A S O N D

Tulipa julia
Tahir Pass, E Anatolia
Dist: E Anatolia
J F M A **M** J J A S O N D

Liliaceae: *Tulipa*

Tulipa undulatifolia
Island of Chios
Dist: W Turkey, C Anatolia, Islands
J F M **A M** J J A S O N D

Fig 362

Fig 363

Tulipa sintenisii (bud)
Nr. Erzurum, NE Anatolia
Dist: C and E Anatolia
J F M **A M** J J A S O N D

Tulipa sintenisii
Nr. Erzurum, NE Anatolia
Dist: C and E Anatolia
J F M **A M** J J A S O N D

Fig 364

145

Liliaceae: *Tulipa*

Tulipa sprengeri
In cultivation in the UK
Dist: N Anatolia (Amasya)
J F M A **M J** J A S O N D

Tulipa sp.
Nr. Erzurum, NE Anatolia
J F M A **M J** J A S O N D

Tulipa wilsoniana
Golestan, NE Iran
Dist: NE Iran
J F M A **M J** J A S O N D

Tulipa systola
Nr. Chelgerd, W Iran
Dist: N and W Iran
J F M A **M J** J A S O N D

Liliaceae: *Tulipa*

Tulipa micheliana
Golestan, NE Iran
Dist: N and NE Iran
J F M **A** M J J A S O N D

Fig 369

Tulipa hoogiana
Golestan, NE Iran
Dist: N and NE Iran
J F M **A** M J J A S O N D

Fig 370

Tulipa ulophylla
Olang, N Iran
Dist: N and C Iran
J F M **A** M J J A S O N D

Fig 371

Liliaceae: *Tulipa*

Tulipa montana
Golestan, NE Iran
Dist: Widespread in Iran
J F **M A** M J J A S O N D

Fig 372

Tulipa montana v. chrysantha
Golestan, NE Iran
Dist: Widespread in Iran
J F **M A** M J J A S O N D

Fig 373

Tulipa montana v. chrysantha
Khosh Yelagh, C Iran
Dist: Widespread in Iran
J F **M A** M J J A S O N D

Fig 374

Liliaceae: *Tulipa*

Tulipa schrenkii
In cultivation in the UK
Dist: W Iran
J F M **A** M J J A S O N D

Tulipa linifolia
In cultivation in the UK
Dist: NE Iran (Golestan)
J F M **A** M J J A S O N D

Tulipa urumiensis
In cultivation in the UK
Dist: NW Iran
J F M **A** M J J A S O N D

Tulipa mucronata
Khomeyn, N Iran
Dist: NW Iran
J F M **A** M J J A S O N D

Tulipa sintenisii
Near Erzurum, NE Anatolia
Dist: C and E Anatolia
J F M **A** M J J A S O N D

Liliaceae: *Erythronium*

Erythronium

The *Erythronium* genus (dog's-tooth violets) is mainly distributed in North America, but two species reach our area, the widespread European *E. dens-canis*, and *E. caucasicum* coming from the Caucasus influence in NE Anatolia.

Erythronium dens-canis (Figs. 380,381)

This pink-flowered *Erythronium* is rare in this area and has only been found in woods in Turkey-in-Europe in the Istanbul area. It is thought that it may now be extinct there.

Erythronium caucasicum (Fig. 382)

This white-flowered species grows in scattered places in woodland in N Iran. As with *E. dens-canis* it has single flowers on short, 15cm, stems and two, broad, spotted leaves.

Erythronium dens-canis
NW Spain
Dist: Turkey-in-Europe
J F M **A M** J J A S O N D

Erythronium dens-canis
N Italy
Dist: Turkey-in-Europe
J F M **A M** J J A S O N D

Erythronium caucasicum
From Nr. Sotschi, Caucasus
Dist; N Iran
J F M **A M** J J A S O N D

Gagea

This is one of the most difficult groups in the family and always causes trouble in identification. With the exception of *Gagea graeca* all species have yellow flowers and are quite similar in appearance. There are many species in both Turkey and Iran, many of them endemic to these countries.

Important characteristics are the presence or absence of bulbils in the axils of the leaves, the number and nature of the basal leaves, the form and number of flowers in the inflorescence and the hairiness of the pedicels.

Gagea graeca (Fig. 383)
This is the only species with white flowers. It forms clumps with each bulb having two linear leaves and stems with 1-5 flowers, which are nodding in bud. It grows in macchie in W Anatolia and the Islands.

Plants with bulbils in the axils of the leaves.

Gagea gageoides (Fig. 384)
This species is easily recognisable owing to the very small flowers and the leafy bulbils in the axils of the leaves. The plant is much branched with a single basal leaf (which may be absent on flowering plants) and many stem leaves, and the small yellow flowers are terminal. It grows on stony hillsides at 1,500-3,000m in E and S Anatolia, and is widespread in Iran.

Gagea granatellii (Fig. 385)
This species also forms clumps and has two linear leaves per bulb, which exceed the umbellate inflorescence. The two stem leaves are more or less opposite and equal the flowers, and they have bunches of blackish, leafy bulbils in their axils. The pedicels of the 2-11 large flowers are densely woolly. It grows in steppe, scrub and open woods in N, Inner and S Anatolia

Gagea bulbifera (not illustrated)
This is another species with many alternate stem-leaves, which are crowded at the base, and have a single leafless bulbil in their axil. There are 1-2 yellow flowers with tepals having a central green stripe on the outside. The plant grows on stony mountain slopes in E Anatolia and rarely in NW Iran.

Gagea bohemica (Fig. 386)
This species does not always have bulbils, but they occasionally occur in the axils of the 2-3 stem leaves. The 1-4 large flowers are yellow inside and greenish outside and the plant grows on rocky slopes at 1,000-2,000m in Outer Anatolia and on the Islands.

Another rare species from SE Anatolia and C Iran, *Gagea tenera*, can also have bulbils, as can small-flowered species from Iran such as *G. ova* and *G. chomutowae*.

Bulbils absent. Basal leaf single and hollow.

Gagea luteoides (Fig. 387)
This species is distinguished by the short length of stem (about 1cm) between the two stem leaves and the start of the umbellate inflorescence. The 2-6 yellow flowers are quite large and have long, 1.5-3cm, pedicels. It occurs on stony hillsides at 1,500-3,000m in S and E Anatolia.

Gagea glacialis (Fig. 388)
This species has two opposite stem leaves, the lower longer than the upper, and 1-4 medium-sized flowers arranged in an umbel. It grows in alpine meadows by melting snow at 2,000-3,000m in E Anatolia.

Gagea fistulosa (Fig. 389)
This is another species found near melting snow in N, C and S Anatolia and in N, NW and W Iran. It is a large plant which grows in wet, grassy places and on bare slopes, and has an umbel of 2-6 large flowers. The two stem leaves are opposite and unequal, and the single, hollow, basal leaf exceeds the scape.

Bulbils absent. Basal leaf single but solid or flat.

Gagea taurica (Fig. 390)
This species has a single, long, linear, basal leaf, which is solid and 5-angled or somewhat channelled, and a whorl of 3-4 stem leaves, the largest of which often exceeds the flowers. It has 1-3 large, pointed flowers, which are yellow inside and green outside, and have pedicels of unequal length. It grows in steppe and on stony hillsides in Inner Anatolia.

Gagea lutea (Fig. 391)
This species is distinguished by its single, very broad leaf (7-15mm), which generally exceeds the flowers. It has two stem leaves which are more or less opposite, and 3-6 large flowers. It is found in open, deciduous woodland on mountains in N Iran.

Gagea fibrosa (Figs. 392, 393)
This species has similar pointed flowers to *Gagea taurica*, but the flower stem is short and the branching often starts near ground level. The basal leaves are linear and flat and considerably exceed

the inflorescence. The 3-5 stem leaves are in a whorl with the longest longer than the flowers. It is found in steppe, on rocky slopes and in oak scrub in S Anatolia and on the Islands.

Gagea confusa (Fig. 394)
This *Gagea* has 1-7 medium-sized flowers which are rather conical in shape, and they are nodding in bud. They are yellow inside and greenish or reddish outside. The single flat, glabrous basal leaf is longer than the inflorescence, and the single stem leaf is shorter than the pedicels. It grows in grassy places by snow patches in E Anatolia and in N, NW and W Iran.

Gagea uliginosa (Fig. 395)
This short-stemmed species has 1-3 bright yellow flowers, which are reddish outside, and the single, narrow stem leaf is shorter than the flowers. It is found in damp mossy places at 2,500-3,500m, mainly in SE Anatolia.

Bulbils absent. Basal leaves 2 or more and approximately equal.

Gagea villosa (Fig. 396)
This species has two linear basal leaves that are D-shaped in section and exceed the inflorescence. The 1-15 narrow-tepalled flowers are of medium size and are often hairy outside at the base. The plants grow in steppe and fields and are widespread in Anatolia, but only found rarely in SW Iran.

Gagea bithynica (Fig. 397)
This species grows in damp places in N Turkey and C and SW Anatolia. The two basal leaves appear with the flowers and are shorter than the inflorescence, and the 2-3 alternate stem leaves are also shorter. The 1-3 medium-sized flowers are yellow with greenish veins.

Gagea peduncularis (Fig. 398)
The two linear basal leaves are glabrous and exceed the inflorescence, and the single stem leaf is equal to or shorter than the flowers. The 1-4 large flowers have long pedicels which are densely woolly above. The tepals are also woolly at the base of the outside. The plant grows on limestone rocks and in coniferous woodland in Turkey-in-Europe, Outer Anatolia and the Islands.

Other species from Iran.

Bulbs forming clumps.
Flowers of medium size.

Gagea olgae (Fig. 399)
This species is recognised by its single, narrow-tepalled flowers, which are orange or purplish on the outside. The narrow basal leaves are of similar length to the flowers, and the 3-5 stem leaves are alternate. It grows in stony places in N and W Iran.

Gagea tenuifolia (Fig. 400)
This species has 1-2 channelled, basal leaves which exceed the inflorescence, and the stem leaves are bract-like and also exceed the flowers. The narrow tepals are pointed and are green and pubescent on the outside. It is found in stony ground in NW and W Iran.

Gagea vegeta (Fig. 401)
This is a low-growing, leafy species with relatively broad leaves that are channelled and ciliate. The few flowers have narrow tepals with long points and they are green on the outside. It grows on stony hillsides in N Iran.

Gagea chomutowae (Fig. 402)
This species has a single, hollow, basal leaf about the same length as the flowers, and the stem leaves, which can have bulbils in their axils, are quite broad (up to 7mm). The few-flowered inflorescence has flowers with rounded, yellow tepals that are greenish on the outside and red tipped. It grows on stony hillsides in N and W Iran.

Individual plants with small to medium flowers.

Gagea stipitata (Fig. 403)
This and the next species often occur together in bare, stony habitats, but *G. stipitata* has smaller, brighter flowers and does not produce bulbils. It has a single, narrow, basal leaf shorter than the inflorescence, and a narrow stem leaf below the lax group of long-pedicelled flowers. It is widespread in stony places in Iran.

Gagea ova (Fig. 404)
This is a shorter plant than the previous species and is distinctive in its pale yellow flowers, the presence of bulbils, and the very long, narrow leaves. It has a single basal leaf and is again widespread in Iran.

Gagea alexeenkoana (Fig. 405)
This *Gagea* is grey-green in appearance. It has a glaucous, channelled, basal leaf longer than the inflorescence, and 2-3 stem leaves which are shorter. The 1-3 flowers have pointed tepals, which are green outside, and the plant is widely distributed in Iran.

Gagea dschungarica (Fig. 406)
This species has very small flowers with rounded, yellow tepals, which are greenish outside and are nodding in bud. It has a single, broad, basal leaf, and stem leaves below the inflorescence. It is widely distributed on stony hills in Iran.

Many other species of *Gagea* occur in both Turkey and Iran, and in total there are about 45 species present in the area.

Liliaceae: *Gagea*

Gagea graeca
Island of Rhodes
Dist: W Anatolia, Islands
J F **M A M** J J A S O N D

Gagea gageoides
Lake Van, SE Anatolia
Dist: E and S Anatolia, Iran (widespread)
J F **M A M** J J A S O N D

Gagea granatellii
Nr. Ibradi, S Anatolia
Dist: N, Inner and S Anatolia
J **F M A M** J J A S O N D

Gagea bohemica
Island of Lesbos
Dist: Outer Anatolia, Islands
J F **M A M** J J A S O N D

Gagea luteoides
Nemrut Dağ, Lake Van, SE Anatolia
Dist: S and E Anatolia
J F **M A M J J A S** O N D

153

Liliaceae: *Gagea*

Gagea glacialis
Kirecli Pass, NE Anatolia
Dist: E Anatolia
J F M A **M J J A S** O N D

Gagea fistulosa
Olang, N Iran
Dist: N, C and S Anatolia, N, NW and W Iran
J F M **A M J J A S** O N D

Gagea taurica
Kop Dağ, Inner Anatolia
Dist: Inner Anatolia
J F M **A M** J J A S O N D

Gagea lutea
Olang, N Iran
Dist: N Iran
J F M **A M** J J A S O N D

Liliaceae: *Gagea*

Gagea fibrosa
Cyprus
Dist: S Anatolia, Islands
J **F M A M J** J A S O N D

Gagea fibrosa
In cultivation in the UK
Dist: S Anatolia, Islands
J **F M A M J** J A S O N D

Gagea confusa
Nr. Shulabad, W Iran
Dist: E Anatolia, N, NW and W Iran
J F M A **M J** J A S O N D

Gagea uliginosa
Nemrut Dağ, Lake Van, SE Anatolia
Dist: S and SE Anatolia
J F M A M **J J** A S O N D

Gagea villosa
Cyprus
Dist: Anatolia (widespread), SW Iran (rare)
J F **M A M** J J A S O N D

Gagea bithynica
Ulu Dağ, Bursa, N Turkey
Dist: N Turkey, C and SW Anatolia
J F M **A M** J J A S O N D

Liliaceae: *Gagea*

Gagea peduncularis
Cyprus
Dist: Turkey-in-Europe, Outer Anatolia, Islands
J F M A M J J A S O N D

Gagea olgae
Golestan, NE Iran
Dist: N and W Iran
J F M A M J J A S O N D

Gagea tenuifolia
Nr. Semirom, W Iran
Dist: Widespread in Iran
J F M A M J J A S O N D

Gagea vegeta
Golestan, N Iran
Dist: N Iran
J F M A M J J A S O N D

Liliaceae: *Gagea*

Gagea chomutowae
Golestan, NE Iran
Dist: N and W Iran
J F **M A** M J J A S O N D

Gagea ova
Nr. Khonsar, W Iran
Dist: Widely distributed in Iran
J F **M A** M J J A S O N D

Gagea alexeenkoana
Nr. Khonsar, W Iran
Dist: Widely distributed in Iran
J F **M A** M J J A S O N D

Gagea stipitata
Nr. Shiraz, SW Iran
Dist: Widely distributed in Iran
J F **M A** M J J A S O N D

Gagea dschungarica
Nr. Khonsar, W Iran
Dist: Widely distributed in Iran
J F **M A** M J J A S O N D

Colchicaceae:

Colchicum speciosum, N Anatolia

Colchicaceae

This family covers the closely related genera of *Colchicum* and *Merendera*. These are what we would call 'autumn crocuses', although they are not, of course, crocuses and many flower in the spring.

Botanically *Merendera* differs from *Colchicum* in having the tepals separated to the base, whereas with *Colchicum* flowers the tepals are joined to form a tube. Some authors do not separate the two groups and put them all in the genus *Colchicum*. Equally the family is often included within *Liliaceae*.

Some members of the family resemble crocuses but *Colchicum* and *Merendera* species have 6 stamens whereas *Crocus* species have 3.

In both genera, flowers appear before, or at the same time as, the leaves. Fruits are formed later in the centre of the leaf rosettes.

Colchicaceae: *Merendera*

Merendera

There are four species of *Merendera* in Turkey and six species in Iran, and almost all of the species in this area are spring-flowering. Most, other than *M. attica,* are found high in the mountains, where there is moisture from melting snow. The leaves of *Merendera* are always visible at flowering time, though as with *Colchicum* they continue to grow after the flowering.

Merendera kurdica (Figs. 408,409)
This species has the largest flowers of any *Merendera* and also has very broad leaves. It flowers as soon as the snow melts on high passes in SE Anatolia and NW Iran.

Merendera trigyna (Fig. 410)
This *Merendera* is much more widespread than the previous species and occurs throughout Anatolia and NW Iran. It has 1-2 medium-sized, pink-purplish flowers with black anthers, and there are 2-3 leaves. It grows in high level pastures and flowers at the edge of snow patches.

Merendera raddeana (Fig. 411)
This species is closely related to *M. trigyna* and by some authors is considered as just a subspecies. It is found in N and W Iran and has solitary, whitish or pale pink flowers with dark yellow to grey anthers. There are two narrow leaves.

Merendera wendelboi (Fig. 412)
This is the most widespread species in western Iran. It has 2-4 pink flowers with yellow anthers, and three long narrow leaves.

Merendera sobolifera (Fig. 413)
This species has stoloniferous tubers which allow it to spread underground, so it usually occurs in patches. It has 1-2 small white or pale pink flowers and three narrow leaves. Again it flowers at high levels and is widespread in Anatolia and NW Iran.

Merendera attica (Fig. 414)
This species occurs at low levels in SW and C Anatolia and is very like some of the *Colchicum* species such as *C. pusillum* and *C. stevenii*. The 3-5 flowers are usually purplish-pink with black anthers, and the four long, narrow leaves are very visible at flowering time. Because of its preferred low limestone hillsides it flowers earlier than other species from November to April.

One other species, *Merendera robusta*, which is not illustrated, grows in N and NE Iran. It has 1-4 large white flowers.

Merendera kurdica
Karabet Pass, SE Anatolia
Dist: SE Anatolia, NW Iran
J F M A M J J A S O N D

Fig 408

Colchicaceae: *Merendera*

Merendera kurdica
Karabet Pass, SE Anatolia
Dist: SE Anatolia, NW Iran
J F M A M J J A S O N D

Fig 409

Fig 410

Merendera trigyna
Karabet Pass, SE Anatolia
Dist: Widespread in Anatolia, NW Iran
J F M **A M** J J A S O N D

Merendera raddeana
Nr. Chelgerd, W Iran
Dist: W and NW Iran
J F M **A M** J J A S O N D

Fig 411

Colchicaceae: *Merendera*

Merendera wendelboi
Nr. Chelgerd, W Iran
Dist: W Iran
J F M A M J J A S O N D

Fig 412

Fig 413

Merendera sobolifera
From Hoşap, SE Anatolia
Dist: Widespread in Anatolia, NW and N Iran
J F M A M J J A S O N D

Merendera attica
Nr. Finike, S Anatolia
Dist: W, S and C Anatolia
J F M A M J J A S O N D

Fig 414

Colchicum

There are many species of *Colchicum* in both Turkey and Iran. They range from species with very large flowers such as *C. bivonae* to really small species such as *C. minutum*. They are divided here into two main groups, those that are autumn-flowering, often with no sign of leaves, and those that are spring-flowering, usually, like *Merendera*, with visible leaves.

Spring-flowering Species

Colchicum szovitsii (Figs. 415, 416)
This species is widespread in damp mountain pastures in C, S and E Anatolia, and in N and W Iran. It has 2-5 medium-sized, white, pink or purple flowers, and often occurs in large numbers. There are 2-3 leaves which are usually quite short at flowering time.

Colchicum triphyllum (Figs. 418, 419)
This species has small, cup-shaped pink flowers with dark anthers. Its three leaves are shorter than the flowers at flowering time, and the plants are found in open ground near melting snow. It is widespread in Anatolia and is also found in NW Iran.

Colchicum burttii (Fig. 417)
This *Colchicum* has similar-sized, white or pale-pink flowers with green-grey or black anthers, and filaments that are hairy at the base. The three leaves are very short at flowering time, and the plants occur in W Turkey and C Anatolia.

Colchicum serpentinum (*C. falcifolium*) (Fig. 420)
The 2-6 white or pink flowers of this species have narrow tepals which give it a starry appearance. The 3-5 leaves are very narrow and short at flowering time, and it is found as a snow-melt plant in C, S and E Anatolia.

Colchicum minutum (Fig. 421)
This tiny *Colchicum* is also starry in appearance with very narrow, pale-pink tepals. It has 3-4 leaves which are much longer than the flowers at flowering time, and it is found in S Anatolia.

Autumn-flowering Species

Large-flowered Species with Tessellated Tepals

Colchicum variegatum (Fig. 422)
The 1-2 flowers of this species are star-shaped and very strongly tessellated. They are usually violet-purple in colour and have purplish-black anthers. It is found in open pine woods or macchie in SW and S Anatolia and on some of the Islands.

Colchicum chalcedonicum (Fig. 423)
This *Colchicum* is similar in appearance to *C. variegatum* and occurs in the Istanbul area in Turkey-in-Europe and NW Turkey. It has single, rosy-purple flowers and grows in stony places in the mountains.

Colchicum bivonae (Fig. 424)
This species has a wide distribution outside Turkey from Italy to the Balkans, and in Turkey it occurs in the European area and in NW Anatolia. It has large, cup-shaped, purple flowers with strongly tessellated tepals.

Colchicum macrophyllum (Fig. 425)
This is another large-flowered, tessellated species with 1-2 wide-opening, rosy-purple flowers with pinkish-purple anthers. It occurs in W Turkey and on some of the Islands in woodland at fairly low levels.

Large flowered Species without Tessellated Tepals

Colchicum speciosum (Fig. 407, 426)
This species, which is well known in cultivation, comes from N Anatolia and N Iran, and it grows in meadows or in open woodland. It has reddish-purple flowers, often with a white throat, and has yellow anthers.

Colchicum bornmuelleri (Fig. 427)
This *Colchicum* is closely related to *C. speciosum* and is often confused with it. It has similar large open flowers which are rosy-purple in colour with a white throat. The most easily recognisable difference is the anthers which are purple-brown in this species, but yellow in *C. speciosum*. It grows in meadows and on forest edges in C Anatolia.

Colchicum cilicicum (Fig. 428)
This *Colchicum* is found in S Anatolia and it has 3-10 bright pink flowers, often with a pale line down the centre of the tepals. The flowers have very long stigmas.

Colchicum turcicum (Fig. 429)
This species occurs in the Bosphorus region of NW Turkey. It has 3-8 red-purple flowers and grows in wet meadows and open fields at low levels.

Colchicum persicum (Fig. 430)
This species has 2-7 pink to purple flowers with yellow anthers. It is found in dry, stony ground in SE Anatolia and W and SW Iran.

Species with Medium-sized Flowers

Colchicum baytopiorum (Fig. 431)
With this species the leaves may be visible at flowering time, but often not, and it has 1-3 bright pink flowers with yellow anthers. The filaments have a swollen, orange-yellow base. It is found in open woodland in SW Anatolia.

Colchicum boissieri (Fig. 434)
The usually single flowers of this species are bright lilac and have yellow anthers on white filaments with a swollen green base. The plant is stoloniferous and grows on clayey hillsides in W and S Anatolia.

Colchicum sanguicolle (Figs. 432,433)
This pink-flowered *Colchicum* can be distinguished from all others by its red cataphyll. This is the membranous sheath that encloses the leaves and inflorescence as they come up through the ground. It is often visible just above the soil surface when the plant is flowering in open pine woods in S Anatolia.

Colchicum kotschyi (Fig. 435)
This is another pink or white-flowered *Colchicum* with filaments with a swollen, orange-yellow base and yellow anthers. The flowers are funnel-shaped and are usually 3-5 in number. It grows at the edge of pine woods in C Anatolia and on dry, rocky slopes in much of Iran.

Colchicum lingulatum (Fig. 436)
This has a north-westerly distribution in Turkey, occuring in the Bosphorus region and W Anatolia. It has funnel-shaped, purplish-pink to white flowers with yellow anthers. In spring it has linear leaves.

Small-flowered Colchicum Species

Colchicum balansae (Figs. 437,438)
Many of the small-flowered species have narrow tepals and are therefore rather starry in appearance, as is this white to pink-flowered species. It has 4-6 flowers with yellow anthers, and grows in macchie in SW and S Anatolia and on some of the Islands.

Colchicum decaisnei (*C. troodii*) (Fig. 440)
This *Colchicum* has 2-6 narrow, funnel-shaped flowers, which are white or pale pink, and it is found in macchie and pine forests in S Anatolia.

Colchicum dolichantherum (Fig. 439)
This is a very similar species with 4-15 white or pink, funnel-shaped flowers. However the anthers are different, with long anthers on short filaments with this species, and the reverse with *C. decaisnei*. *C. dolichantherum* grows in damp places in S Anatolia.

Colchicum stevenii (Fig. 441)
This is a starry, bright pink species which often occurs in groups. It has 2-5 funnel-shaped flowers and the 4-8 narrow, green leaves are visible at the time of flowering. It occurs at low levels in dry, rocky places in W and S Anatolia.

Colchicum pusillum (Fig. 442)
This species is very similar to *C. stevenii* but is only known from the Islands in this area, notably Tilos. It has 1-4 starry, pink flowers with purplish-black anthers, and again the leaves are visible at the time of flowering.

Colchicum micranthum (Fig. 443)
This is the only small-flowered species in NW Turkey and Turkey-in-Europe, and the pale pink, starry flowers appear without the leaves in meadows at low levels.

Colchicum umbrosum (Fig. 444)
This *Colchicum* from N Anatolia has 1-3 white to purplish-pink flowers which start funnel-shaped but open fully to a starry form. It grows in meadows and moist open woodland.

Other species in Turkey include the autumn-flowering *C. inundatum*, *C. heldreichii* and *C. paschei*. In Iran other species such as *C. crocifolium*, *C. schimperi*, *C. varians* and *C. freynii*, all spring-flowering, are mainly found in the west.

Colchicaceae: *Colchicum*

Colchicum szovitsii
Karabet Pass, SE Anatolia
Dist: Widely distributed in Anatolia, N and W Iran
J **F M A M** J J A S O N D

Colchicum szovitsii
Gembos Yayla, S Anatolia
Dist: Widely distributed in Anatolia, N and W Iran
J **F M A M** J J A S O N D

Colchicum burttii
Nr. Akseki, S Anatolia
Dist: W Turkey, S and C Anatolia
J **F M** A M J J A S O N D

Colchicum triphyllum
Nr. Ibradi, S Anatolia
Dist: W, C and S Anatolia, NW Iran
J **F M A M** J J A S O N D

Colchicum triphyllum
Nr. Rasht, Iran
Dist: W, C and S Anatolia, NW Iran
J **F M A M** J J A S O N D

Colchicaceae: *Colchicum*

Colchicum serpentinum
Ala Dağ, Adana S Anatolia
Dist: C, S and E Anatolia
J **F M A** M J J A **S** O N D

Fig 420

Fig 421

Colchicum minutum
Nr. Akseki, S Anatolia
Dist: S Anatolia
J **F M** A M J J A S O N D

Colchicum variegatum
Nr. Antalya, S Anatolia
Dist: SW and S Anatolia, Islands
J F M A M J J A **S O N** D

Fig 422

Colchicaceae: *Colchicum*

Colchicum chalcedonicum
Yakaçik, NW Turkey
Dist: Turkey-in-Europe, NW Turkey
J F M A M J J A **S O** N D

Fig 423

Colchicum bivonae
Greece
Dist: W Turkey, Islands
J F M A M J J A **S O** N D

Fig 424

Colchicum macrophyllum
Island of Rhodes
Dist: SW Anatolia, Islands
J F M A M J J A **S O** N D

Fig 425

167

Colchicaceae: *Colchicum*

Colchicum speciosum
Ilgaz Dağ, N Anatolia
Dist: N and E Anatolia
J F M A M J J A **S O N** D

Fig 426

Fig 427

Colchicum bornmuelleri
In cultivation at RBG, Edinburgh
Dist: C Anatolia
J F M A M J **J A S O N** D

Colchicum cilicicum
In cultivation at RBG, Edinburgh
Dist: S Anatolia
J F M A M J J A **S O N** D

Fig 428

Colchicaceae: *Colchicum*

Colchicum turcicum
Tekir Dağ, NW Turkey
Dist: NW Turkey
J F M A M J J A **S O N** D

Colchicum persicum
Persepolis, W Iran
Dist: S Anatolia, W and SW Iran
J F M A M J J A **S O N** D

Colchicum baytopiorum
Termessos, S Anatolia
Dist: S and SW Anatolia
J F M A M J J A S **O N** D

Colchicum sanguicolle
Tahtali Dağ, S Anatolia
Dist: S and SW Anatolia
J F M A M J J A S **O N** D

Colchicaceae: *Colchicum*

Colchicum sanguicolle
Tahtali Dağ, S Anatolia
Dist: S and SW Anatolia
J F M A M J J A S **O N D**

Colchicum boissieri
S Greece
Dist: W and S Anatolia
J F M A M J J A **S O N** D

Colchicum kotschyi
In cultivation in the UK
Dist: Inner Anatolia
J F M A M J J **A S O N D**

Colchicum lingulatum
Greece
Dist: NW Turkey, W Anatolia
J F M A M J J **A S O N** D

Colchicaceae: *Colchicum*

Colchicum balansae
Tahtali Dağ, S Anatolia
Dist: SW and S Anatolia
J F M A M J J **A S O** N D

Fig 437

Fig 438

Colchicum balansae
Marmaris Peninsula, SW Anatolia
Dist: SW and S Anatolia
J F M A M J J **A S O** N D

Fig 439

Colchicum dolichantherum
Tahtali Dağ, S Anatolia
Dist: S Anatolia
J F M A M J J A **S O N** D

Colchicum decaisnei
Nr. Kumluca, S Anatolia
Dist: S Anatolia
J F M A M J J A **S O N** D

Fig 440

171

Colchicaceae: *Colchicum*

Colchicum stevenii
Finike, S Anatolia
Dist: W and S Anatolia
J F M A M J J A S **O N D**

Colchicum pusillum
Crete
Dist: Islands (Tilos)
J F M A M J J A S **O N D**

Colchicum micranthum
Nr. Istanbul, NW Turkey
Dist: NW Turkey
J F M A M J J **A S O N** D

Colchium umbrosum
From Lake Abant, Bolu, N Anatolia
Dist: N Anatolia
J F M A M J J **A S O N** D

Amaryllidaceae

The *Amaryllis* family is close to *Liliaceae* but is distinguished by having flowers with an inferior, rather than superior, ovary (see p.9). The best known genus in this group is *Narcissus*, which is barely represented in this area with only two species. For Turkey and Iran the most important genera are *Sternbergia* and *Galanthus*.

Amaryllidaceae: *Sternbergia*

Sternbergia

This is an attractive family with single yellow or white flowers which look rather like a large *Crocus*, but they have six stamens not three. Most are autumn-flowering.

Sternbergia lutea (Figs. 445, 446)
This is the most widely distributed species, but in our area it is only found in W Anatolia and the Islands. It has very large, deep yellow flowers, which appear without the leaves in the autumn. The leaves often appear later and are broadly linear, erect and bright green. It is usually found in cultivated areas such as olive groves and vineyards.

Sternbergia sicula (Fig. 447)
This is closely related to *S. lutea* and is sometimes considered a subspecies of it. However it is generally smaller in size with dark green leaves with a greyish stripe, and these are visible at flowering time and lie on the ground, though not fully developed. It usually grows in dry, rocky places in the same regions as *S. lutea*.

Sternbergia clusiana (Fig. 448)
This is another large-flowered species with deep yellow, short-stemmed flowers. It is widely distributed in this area, occurring in W, S and E Anatolia and the Islands, and in W Iran. The grey-green leaves are wider than with other species (up to 18mm), but are not visible at flowering time. It grows on stony hillsides and in open pine forests and flowers in late autumn.

Sternbergia colchiciflora (Fig. 449)
This is a much smaller yellow-flowered species with narrow, dark green leaves. The flowers are sessile (no stem) and are found in autumn in open stony areas of Outer Anatolia, and possibly in N Iran (Golestan).

Sternbergia fischeriana (Fig. 450)
This is the only yellow, spring-flowering *Sternbergia*, and it grows in stony scrub and open woods in S and SW Anatolia and N and W Iran. The flowers are pale yellow and short stemmed and the leaves are visible at flowering time.

Sternbergia candida (Figs. 451, 452)
S. candida is easily distinguished from other species as it has large, white flowers produced in the spring. It is very localised and is restricted to the Fethiye area of SW Anatolia, where it grows in scrub and open stony places.

Sternbergia lutea
Island of Rhodes
Dist: W Anatolia, Islands
J F M A M J J A **S O N** D

Sternbergia lutea
Muğla, SW Anatolia
Dist: W Anatolia, Islands
J F M A M J J A **S O N** D

Amaryllidaceae: *Sternbergia*

Sternbergia sicula
Island of Chios
Dist: W Anatolia, Islands
J F M A M J J A S **O N** D

Sternbergia clusiana
Nr. Kemaliye, C Anatolia
Dist: W, S and E Anatolia, Islands, W and S Iran
J F M A M J J A S **O N** D

Sternbergia colchiciflora
Nr. Gaziantep, S Anatolia
Dist: Outer Anatolia
J F M A M J J A **S O N** D

Sternbergia fischeriana
Bozburun, SW Anatolia
Dist: S and SW Anatolia, N and W Iran
J **F M** A M J J A S O N D

Amaryllidaceae: *Sternbergia*/*Leucojum*

Fig 451

Sternbergia candida
Nr. Fethiye, SW Anatolia
Dist: SW Anatolia
J F M A M J J A S O N D

Fig 452

Sternbergia candida
In cultivation in the UK
Dist: SW Anatolia
J F M A M J J A S O N D

Leucojum

The snowflakes are only represented in this area by the summer snowflake (*Leucojum aestivum*). In general they are similar in appearance to snowdrops.

Leucojum aestivum (Figs. 453, 454)

This is the largest of the snowflakes with stems 60-90cm tall and clusters of 2-5 bell-shaped, white flowers. It is a plant of wet meadows in N Turkey, S Anatolia and N Iran.

Fig 453

Leucojum aestivum
Nr. Eğridir, S Anatolia
Dist: N Turkey, S Anatolia, N Iran
J F **M A M J** J A S O N D

Fig 454

Leucojum aestivum
Nr. Eğridir, S Anatolia
Dist: N Turkey, S Anatolia, N Iran
J F **M A M J** J A S O N D

Galanthus

Snowdrops attract considerable horticultural interest even though the range of wild species is quite limited. Turkey is the epicentre for *Galanthus* species with at least nine found there and one also in Iran. Flowering time is an important characteristic as are form and colour of the leaves, and the green spotting on the inner petals of the flowers.

Plants Autumn-flowering

Galanthus peshmenii (Fig. 455)
This is the main autumn-flowering species in the area. It flowers without the leaves in October and November in the Antalya area of S Anatolia, and is found at low levels in macchie or amongst limestone rocks. It has been confused in the past with *Galanthus reginae-olgae*, which is another autumn-flowering species from Greece.

A related species, *G. cilicicus*, flowers from November to January and is only found in the Içel region of S Anatolia. The leaves are visible at flowering time, and the plant grows in similar habitats to *G. peshmenii*.

Plants Spring-flowering. Leaves green.

Galanthus woronowii (Fig. 456)
This species has broad, glossy, bright green leaves, which are recurved at the tips. The inner petals of the flower have a small green spot at the apex. It only occurs in the Pontic Alps in NE Anatolia, growing at relatively low levels (100-500m) in damp deciduous woodland and rocky crevices.

Galanthus fosteri (Fig. 457)
This is another species with broad, bright green leaves, which grows at higher levels (800-1,500m) in N, C and S Anatolia. The inner petals have separate green spots at their base and apex. It grows in rocky areas at the edge of deciduous forests.

Galanthus transcaucasicus (Fig. 458)
This is the only *Galanthus* species known for certain from Iran. It has darker leaves than the similar *G. woronowii* and inner petals with a single apical spot. It is a mountain species growing in deciduous woodland at 1,600-2,000m in N Iran.

A species from Azerbaijan, *G. lagodechianus*, may also occur in NW Iran.

Galanthus rizehensis (Fig. 459)
This is another snowdrop from the Pontic Mountains in NE Anatolia. It has linear leaves with a conspicuous midrib, and the inner petals have a single green spot at the apex. It grows in damp, deciduous woodland.

Plants Spring-flowering. Leaves glaucous.

Galanthus plicatus ssp. byzantinus (Fig. 460)
This species has narrow, glaucous leaves which have margins that are folded back when they first appear. The inner petals have separate green patches at the base and apex. It grows in open grassy places or forest margins at relatively low levels in NW Turkey. Another form (*ssp. plicatus*), which only has a green spot at the apex of the petals, is also recognised.

Galanthus elwesii (Figs. 461,462)
This species has rather wider, glaucous leaves which are flat in bud, and flowers with separate green patches at base and apex of the inner petals. These sometimes merge so the inner petals are largely green. It grows at higher levels (1,000-1,800m) in open scrub and coniferous forest in SW and S Anatolia.

Galanthus gracilis (Fig. 463)
This snowdrop has very narrow, upright, glaucous leaves and again has flowers with green patches at the base and apex of the inner petals. It grows in much wetter places in meadows or in damp leaf mould under trees. It is found in NW Turkey and W and SW Anatolia and the Islands.

Galanthus alpinus (Fig. 464)
This is a small snowdrop with linear, glaucous leaves which have a conspicuous midrib. It most resembles *G. elwesii* but has a smaller green mark at the apex of the inner petals, and is in general a smaller plant. However in the wild it is found in a completely different area, and is the most common, glaucous-leaved species from NE Anatolia.

Galanthus koenenianus (Fig. 465)
This species is only found in the Gümüşhane region of NE Anatolia, growing in damp, deciduous woodland, often under hazel bushes, on the N side of the Pontic Alps. The glaucous leaves are shiny, and the inner petals of the flowers have a u-shaped green mark at the apex.

Galanthus nivalis (Fig. 466)
This very widespread European snowdrop has narrow, glaucous leaves, and it has a green spot only at the apex of the inner petals. It is a low level species found on scrubby hillsides and in light woodland in NW Turkey.

Other very localised species occurring in Turkey include *G. trojanus* and *G. krasnovii*.

Amaryllidaceae: *Galanthus*

Galanthus peshmenii
Tahtali Dağ, S Anatolia
Dist: S Anatolia (Antalya)
J F M A M J J A S **O N D**

Galanthus woronowii
Yesilköy, NE Anatolia
Dist: NE Anatolia
J F **M A** M J J A S O N D

Galanthus fosteri
From nr. Adana, S Anatolia
Dist: N, C and S Anatolia
J **F M A** M J J A S O N D

Galanthus transcaucasicus
Olang, N Iran
Dist: N Iran
J **F M A** M J J A S O N D

Amaryllidaceae: *Galanthus*

Galanthus rizehensis
Muratli, Nr Borçka, NE Anatolia
Dist: NE Anatolia
J F M A M J J A S O N D

Galanthus plicatus* ssp. *byzantinus
Bolu, NW Turkey
Dist: NW Turkey
J F M A M J J A S O N D

Galanthus elwesii
Nr. Akseki, S Anatolia
Dist: SW and S Anatolia
J F M A M J J A S O N D

Galanthus elwesii
Nr. Akseki, S Anatolia
Dist: SW and S Anatolia
J F M A M J J A S O N D

179

Amaryllidaceae: *Galanthus*

Fig 463

Fig 464

Galanthus gracilis
Nr. Tekir Dağ, NW Turkey
Dist: NW Turkey, W and SW Anatolia, Islands
J **F M A** M J J A S O N D

Galanthus alpinus
Nr Çamlihemşin, NE Anatolia
Dist: NE Anatolia
J **F M A** M J J A S O N D

Fig 465

Fig 466

Galanthus koenenianus
In cultivation in the UK
Dist: NE Anatolia
J **F M A** M J J A S O N D

Galanthus nivalis
Istanbul area, NW Turkey
Dist: NW Turkey
J **F M A** M J J A S O N **D**

Ixiolirion

There is only one species in this area.

Ixiolirion tataricum (Figs. 467, 468)
This blue-flowered species is distributed widely in Iran and E Anatolia. It is usually found in cultivated land but also on rocky limestone slopes.

Narcissus

The very extensive daffodil family is hardly represented in Turkey and Iran with only two species present. Other species are cultivated in the area and some escape and can become naturalised, but these are not covered here.

Narcissus tazetta (Fig. 469)
This distinctive, multi-headed *Narcissus* is normally found in marshy areas at low altitudes, but it also occurs in rocky coastal places, macchie and open pine forests. It flowers very early in the year and is found in E Anatolia and the Islands. In Iran it has only been reported from the south, where it may be naturalised rather than native. A yellow-flowered form, *ssp. aureus*, occurs in Turkey-in-Europe and on islands such as Rhodes.

Narcissus serotinus (Fig. 470)
This is another low level species growing in damp places on stony hillsides. This small *Narcissus* is autumn-flowering and is very strongly scented. Although it is widespread in the Mediterranean region, it is rare in its only sites in W and S Anatolia and the Islands.

Pancratium

This is another genus with only one species present in our area.

Pancratium maritimum (Figs. 471, 472)
As the name suggests this is a coastal species growing on sandy beaches and in sand dune systems. It flowers in the summer and is found in Turkey-in-Europe, Outer Anatolia and the Islands.

Ungernia

This is a poorly known genus, though there are two species widely distributed in Iran, *Ungernia trisphaera* and *U. flava*. The leaves of these bulbous plants are produced in spring, but they have died away before the umbels of 6-8 flowers appear in July and August. *Ungernia trisphaera* has brownish flowers and those of *U. flava* are yellowish.

The species illustrated is **Ungernia severzovii (Fig. 473)** from southern Kazakhstan but it is similar in appearance to *U. trisphaera* and gives an impression of the genus

Amaryllidaceae: *Ixiolirion/Narcissus*

Ixiolirion tataricum
Nr. Ercek, E Anatolia
Dist: E Anatolia, widespread in Iran
J F M **A M J** J A S O N D

Ixiolirion tataricum
Tooran, N Iran
Dist: E Anatolia, widespread in Iran
J F M **A M J** J A S O N D

Narcissus tazetta
Nr. Antalya, S Anatolia
Dist: Outer and E Anatolia, Turkey-in-Europe, Islands, S Iran
J F M A M J J A S O **N D**

Narcissus serotinus
Nr. Marmaris, W Anatolia
Dist: W and S Anatolia, Islands
J F M A M J J A **S O N** D

Amaryllidaceae: *Pancratium/Ungernia*

Pancratium maritimum
Island of Rhodes
Dist: Turkey-in-Europe, Outer Anatolia, Islands
J F M A M **J J A S O** N D

Pancratium maritimum
Island of Rhodes
Dist: Turkey-in-Europe, Outer Anatolia, Islands
J F M A M **J J A S O** N D

Ungernia severzovii
S Kazakhstan
Dist: not in our area
J F M A M J **J A** S O N D

Iridaceae:

Iris paradoxa f. choschab, Nr Van, SE Anatolia

Iridaceae

The *Iris* family, which includes large genera such as *Iris, Crocus, Romulea* and *Gladiolus*, has many interesting, and sometimes spectacular, species in this area. Turkey, with Greece, is the home of *Crocus* species, and there are more than 35 recognised in the area, several with multiple sub-species also.

The *Iris* group is very strongly represented with Juno, Oncocyclus and Reticulate Irises which are virtually unrepresented in the general European area. These come from the eastern and middle-eastern influences on the Turkish and Iranian flora.

Iridaceae: *Iris*

Iris

The genus *Iris* is very extensive in this area and there are many representatives of the five main types, including some that are really spectacular.

Irises from the region can be grouped in five main types:

1. The Limniris Group (e.g. *Iris sibirica*)
2. The Bearded Iris Group (e.g. *Iris germanica*)
3. The Oncocyclus Group (e.g. *Iris iberica*)
4. The Reticulata Group (e.g. *Iris reticulata*)
5. The Juno Iris Group (e.g. *Iris caucasica*)

Many of the Irises can be recognised from the photographs and need little further description, but others are more difficult, though they are often readily separated on the basis of their geographical distribution.

The flower structure of the *Iris* is distinctive, with the three outer segments (the falls) consisting of a glabrous or bearded claw and the often deflexed lamina with a raised central crest and signal patch. The inner segments (the standards) are often erect and well-developed but can be much smaller than the falls.

1. The Limniris Group

This group has a rhizomatous root. The falls are glabrous.

Iris pseudacorus (not illustrated)
This widespread and familiar *Iris* is found in all areas of Turkey except the east, and in the Caspian area of N Iran. It grows in wet places by streams and ponds and in water meadows.

Iris sibirica (Fig. 476)
This is another water-loving *Iris* but is found in this area only in NE Anatolia.

Iris spuria ssp. musulmanica (Fig. 477)
This tall *Iris* (up to 1m) has pale blue flowers and is found in damp meadows and on salty plains in Inner Anatolia and in N, NW and S Iran.

Iris orientalis (Fig. 478)
This is another species growing in damp meadows and marshes in suitable places in W, C and S Anatolia and the Islands. It is similar to the previous species but has white flowers with a large yellow signal patch in the centre of the falls.

Iris kerneriana (Fig. 481)
This yellow-flowered species is found in scrub and open pine forests in N Anatolia. It is short in stature (20-45cm) and has 2-4 terminal flowers.

Iris sintenisii (Fig. 479)
This *Iris* is again short-stemmed (8-25cm) with quite narrow violet flowers with falls which are prominently veined. It grows in grassy places and light woodland in the western half of N Anatolia.

Iris songarica (Fig. 480)
This small, pale blue *Iris* grows on very dry, stony hillsides and on sandy plains in W and SW Iran. It has very narrow leaves and stems with 1 or 2 flowers.

Iris unguicularis ssp. carica (Fig. 482)
This widely distributed Mediterranean species grows in SW Anatolia and the Islands. The form in Turkey, ssp. *carica*, has lavender blue flowers with darker veins. The leaves are very narrow (1-2mm) and the plant forms dense clumps. A similar form with wider leaves (2-5mm) is found in the Hatay area (ssp. *syriaca*).

Iris lazica (Fig. 483)
This species is sometimes considered to be a subspecies of *I. unguicularis,* and is certainly closely related. It has larger, deep-lavender flowers and much broader leaves (1–1.5cm), and is found in dry scrub and open pine woods in W and S Anatolia.

Iris masia (Fig. 484)
This *Iris* from the eastern part of S Anatolia has 6-8 narrow leaves which often exceed the flowers. Flower colour is variable from pale to dark violet-blue with the falls strongly veined on a whitish ground. It grows in fields, often in volcanic steppe.

2. The Bearded Iris Group

This is another group with a rhizome, but the falls of the flowers have a strongly bearded claw.

Iris germanica (Fig. 485)
This very well-known and widely distributed *Iris* is usually associated with areas of habitation and it never occurs in truly wild situations. In Turkey it grows mainly in Outer Anatolia and the Islands and is often found in cemeteries.

Iris mesopotamica (Fig. 486)
This species is very similar to *I. germanica* but it is paler in colour and has a white beard. It is commonly planted in cemeteries in the Hatay area of S Anatolia, but occurs wild in the hills south of Antakya.

Iridaceae: *Iris*

Iris albicans (Fig. 487)

This is another *Iris* associated with graveyard sites and it has large white flowers with a yellow beard. It is widespread in Turkey.

Iris purpureobractea (Fig. 488)

The distinctive feature of this *Iris* is the large purplish bracts. As with most Irises in this group the flowering stem is branched, and the flowers are pale yellow with falls often suffused with purple or blue. It is an endemic species from rocky places in N, W and C Anatolia.

Iris imbricata (Fig. 489)

This is another pale-yellow flowered, bearded *Iris* which comes from the northern side of the Alborz Mountains in N Iran.

Iris taochia (Figs. 490, 491)

This short-stemmed *Iris* (15-30cm) comes from NE Anatolia where it grows on dry, open, rocky slopes. The flowers vary in colour from purple to yellow.

Iris schachtii (Fig. 492)

This is another yellow-flowered species growing on stony hills in C Anatolia. It is related to *I. taochia* but is generally smaller, and the falls are often suffused with brown.

Iris aphylla (Fig. 493)

This is a short-stemmed, purple *Iris* with a distinctive white beard, which has been found recently in NE Anatolia. It grows in rocky places in the Ardahan area.

Iris suaveolens (Fig. 494)

This is another short-stemmed *Iris* with 1-2, purple, yellow or bicoloured flowers. It has a western distribution in N, NW and W Turkey and the Islands and occurs on rocky hillsides.

Iris attica (Fig. 495)

This species is very similar to *I. suaveolens* with a single flower usually with brownish falls. It grows in oak scrub in NW Anatolia.

3. The Oncocyclus Group

This group of Irises is centred in the Middle East region, and in Turkey they are only found in the south and east, particularly the south-east; the range then extends to north and west Iran.

They have rhizomes and all are plants of hot, dry soils with short, usually falcate (sickle-shaped) leaves. The flowers are very large on short, unbranched stems, and they have a large brown or black signal patch on the falls.

Iris gatesii (Fig. 496)

This species occurs on dry slopes in SE and S Anatolia, particularly around Mardin, and it has brownish-purple veined falls on a whitish or creamy-yellow background. The signal patch is quite small and the veins are very fine.

Iris kirkwoodii (Figs. 497, 498)

This *Iris* is quite tall for the group (up to 60cm) and grows in the Amanus region of S Anatolia. It has falls with strong purple spots and veins on a whitish background and the standards are similarly marked.

Iris iberica (Figs. 500–504)

This *Iris* has two subspecies, **ssp. elegantissima** (Figs. 500, 501) and **ssp. lycotis**. (Figs. 502, 503). The former is found in E Anatolia and NW Iran in short turf or steppe conditions. It is up to 30cm tall and has falcate leaves. The large flowers have falls which are heavily spotted and veined with brownish-purple on a white background and the standards are usually white. It is occasionally found in a yellow form (Fig. 504).

The *ssp. lycotis* has much darker-looking flowers, with both standards and falls heavily spotted and veined with dark purple on a white ground. It grows on open stony ground in the extreme SE of Anatolia (Hakkari region), but is more common in the Zagros Mountains of W Iran.

Iris paradoxa (Choschab Form) (Figs. 474, 499)

This species is quite different in appearance with small, narrow falls which are totally covered with a dense, blackish-purple, violet or brown beard, with a white V-shaped mark in the centre. The standards are much larger and are white with strong purple veins. It is found in mountain steppe in SE Anatolia and NW Iran.

Iris barnumae (Figs. 516–520)

This beautiful *Iris* has three forms, **f. barnumae** (Fig. 516), **f. urmiensis** (Figs. 518, 519) and **f. protonyma** (Fig. 517). The *barnumae* form is the most widespread with deep purple flowers with a narrow yellow band on the falls, and it is found on dry hillsides in SE Anatolia and NW Iran.

The *urmiensis* form is bright yellow and it grows mainly in the region of Lake Urmiah in NW Iran, but it is also found locally in SE Anatolia.

The *protonyma* form has dark purple falls and purple-violet standards and is another form found in NW Iran.

Finally there is another subspecies of *I. barnumae*, **ssp. demawendica** (Fig. 520), which grows in the Alborz Mountains of N Iran. This is a coarser plant with broader, more erect leaves and purple flowers, and it grows on open, stony hillsides.

Iris sari (Figs. 505–507)

This endemic species is probably the most variable of the Oncocyclus Irises. It has falcate leaves and large flowers on short stems and it is found on dry steppe in Inner and S Anatolia. The flower has narrow falls which are veined in red-brown, purple or chocolate on a yellowish ground, and they have a large median blotch of maroon, brown or purple. The standards are large and usually darker than the falls and are veined with reddish or bluish purple.

Iris meda (Figs. 508–511)

This very variable *Iris* has yellow, cream or white standards veined with brown, and smaller falls with a noticeable, yellow, bearded centre and often brown tips. It is found at the edges of fields in the Kordestan area of NW Iran.

Also in this area are a very variable range of Irises that may well be hybrids. Four examples are shown (**Figs. 512–515**), one of which (**Fig. 512**) clearly has *Iris acutiloba* as one of the parents. All have very dense, purple beards on the falls.

Iris acutiloba ssp. *lineolata* (Figs. 521–523)

This is the most widely distributed member of this group growing in Iran, where it is found on dry, stony hillsides in the N, W and SW. The flowers of this *Iris*, particularly those from the Zanjan area, are much more pointed in appearance and the falls are whitish with brown or grey veins, and a blackish signal patch.

4. The Reticulata Group

Irises within this group are bulbous and have long, narrow leaves, which are often sharply angled, and short-stemmed flowers.

Iris reticulata (Figs. 524–528)

The wild forms of this commonly cultivated *Iris* show much of the variation that is present in the cultivars. Flower colour and size are very variable and flowers can be blue, violet or purple, usually with a yellow central ridge on the falls. Three main varieties are recognised, *v. reticulata*, *v. bakeriana* and *v. hyrcana*. The most widespread form, **v. reticulata** (**Figs. 524, 525**), is found in mountain grassland and on stony slopes in E Anatolia and NW and W Iran. It often flowers close to melting snow and is distinguished from *v. bakeriana* by its 4-angled leaves.

The variety **v. bakeriana** (**Fig. 526**) has more grooved leaves with 8 ribs. The flowers are usually dark violet with a whitish claw and no yellow median ridge. It grows in the Mardin region of E Anatolia and in W Iran.

The variety **v. hyrcana** (**Figs. 527, 528**) is a form from the Caspian area of NW Iran which has blue flowers with quite broad falls with a very strong yellow median ridge.

Iris histrioides (Fig. 529)

This species has bright blue flowers with conspicuous, dark blue blotches around the yellow median ridge on the falls. As with the next species the bracts are papery in contrast to the green bracts of *I. reticulata*. It occurs in N Anatolia in the Amasya region and is found on open, stony slopes and in pine forests.

Iris histrio (Fig. 530)

The flowers of this species are pale blue and the falls are blue-blotched on a cream or very pale blue ground. It flowers as the snow melts in the Taurus and Amanus mountains of S Anatolia.

Iris pamphylica (Fig. 531)

This is a rather taller species found in open forest and scrub in the Antalya area of S Anatolia. It has 4-angled leaves and the flowers are bi-coloured. The falls are brownish-purple with a yellow, purple-spotted median ridge, and the standards are blue.

Iris danfordiae (Fig. 532, 533)

This well-known species is endemic to Turkey and is widely distributed in N, C and S Anatolia. It flowers on stony slopes near to melting snow, and its bright yellow flowers distinguish it from all other species in this area.

5. The Juno Iris Group

This is another bulbous group but the leaves are quite broad and are arranged in two opposite rows and they are often falcate. The flower falls have a central crest but are not bearded.

Iris aucheri (Fig. 534)

This leafy species has 3-6 blue to white flowers with a distinct yellow or cream crest in the centre of the falls. It can be up to 40cm tall and grows on rocky hillsides in S and E Anatolia and NW Iran.

Iris caucasica (Figs. 475, 535, 536)

This yellow-flowered Juno is about 15cm tall and has 1-4 greenish-yellow flowers with a darker yellow or orange crest on the falls. Two subspecies are recognised, **ssp. caucasica** with leaves with ciliate margins, coming from NE Anatolia, and **ssp. turcica** with smooth leaf margins and coming from Inner and SE Anatolia.

Iris pseudocaucasica (Fig. 537)
This species is very similar to *I. caucasica* but is distinguished by the winged claw which is clearly raised above the falls. It grows in scree and on stony slopes in SE Anatolia and N and NW Iran.

Iris kopetdagensis (Fig. 538)
This is a quite tall, yellow-flowered *Iris* from NE Iran and it can have up to 9 flowers. The narrow, yellow falls have a darker yellow centre and the standards are reduced to bristle-like structures. It grows in dry steppe and on stony mountain slopes.

Iris drepanophylla (not illustrated)
This is a similar species to *I. kopetdagensis* with greenish-yellow flowers and ciliate leaves. It grows in the southern part of the Khorasan area of E Iran.

Iris fosteriana (Fig. 539)
This distinctive Juno *Iris* from N and NE Iran has single flowers with pale yellow falls and a broad, dark yellow centre. The relatively large standards are purple and strongly deflexed. It grows, often in large numbers, on dry, stony hillsides.

Iris stenophylla (Figs. 540–542)
This is a violet-blue flowered Juno with solitary flowers. It has a very short stem, and flowers as the leaves begin to appear. It grows in macchie and in stony ground in S Anatolia.

Iris galatica (Figs. 543, 544)
This species is variable in flower colour and the short-stemmed, 1-2 flowers can be reddish-purple, greenish-yellow or silvery-purple in colour with a yellow or orange crest on the falls. The bracts are both green. It grows in steppe or scrub in C Anatolia.

Iris persica (Figs. 545–547)
This species is similar to *I. galatica* and the 1-4 flowers are silvery-grey, dull yellow, brown or greyish-green. The tube of the flowers is relatively long and the falls are often purple tipped. One bract is green and the other is membranous. The plant is found on stony ground or in scrub in S and SE Anatolia.

Iris hymenospatha (not illustrated)
This species from W Iran is closely related to *I. persica* which does not occur in Iran. It has membranous bracts and flowers with whitish or creamish falls with a yellow central area edged with purple. The standards are narrow and deflexed.

Iris caucasica
Çam Pass, NE Anatolia
Dist: NE Anatolia
J F M A M **J** J A S O N D

Iridaceae: *Iris*

Fig 476

Iris sibirica
Nr. Ardahan, NE Anatolia
Dist: NE Anatolia
J F M A M **J J** A S O N D

Fig 477

Iris spuria ssp. musulmanica
Lake Van, SE Anatolia
Dist: Inner Anatolia, NW and S Iran
J F M A **M J J** A S O N D

Fig 478

Iris orientalis
Nr. Eğridir, S Anatolia
Dist: W, C and S Anatolia, Islands
J F M A **M J** J A S O N D

Fig 479

Iris sintenisii
Abant, N Anatolia
Dist: N Anatolia
J F M A M **J J** A S O N D

Iridaceae: *Iris*

Iris songarica
Nr. Semirom, W Iran
Dist: W and S Iran
J F M **A M J** J A S O N D

Iris kerneriana
In cultivation in the UK
Dist: N Anatolia
J F M A **M J J** A S O N D

Iris unguicularis v. carica
Nr. Muğla, SW Anatolia
Dist: W and S Anatolia
J F **M A M** J J A S O N D

Iris lazica
Nr. Trabzon, NE Anatolia
Dist: NE Anatolia
J F **M A M** J J A S O N D

Iridaceae: *Iris*

Iris masia
Nr. Antalya, S Anatolia
Dist: S Anatolia
J F **M A M** J J A S O N D

Iris germanica
Nr. Maraş, S Anatolia
Dist: Outer Anatolia, Islands
J F **M A M** J J A S O N D

Iris mesopotamica
Nr. Antakya, S Anatolia
Dist: S Anatolia
J F **M A M** J J A S O N D

Iris albicans
Nr. Antalya, S Anatolia
Dist: Widespread in Turkey
J **F M A M** J J A S O N D

Iridaceae: *Iris*

Fig 488

Iris purpureobractea
Nr. Eğridir, C Anatolia
Dist: N, W and C Anatolia
J F M **A M** J J A S O N D

Fig 489

Iris imbricata
Chalus Valley, N Iran
Dist: N Iran
J F M A **M J** J A S O N D

Fig 490

Iris taochia
Tortum Valley, NE Anatolia
Dist: NE Anatolia
J F M A **M J** J A S O N D

Fig 491

Iris taochia
Tortum Valley, NE Anatolia
Dist: NE Anatolia
J F M A **M J** J A S O N D

193

Iridaceae: *Iris*

Iris schachtii
Nr. Konya, C Anatolia
Dist: C Anatolia
J F M A **M J** J A S O N D

Iris aphylla
Nr. Ardahan, NE Anatolia
Dist: NE Anatolia
J F M A **M J** J A S O N D

Iris suaveolens
Island of Chios
Dist: N, NW and W Turkey, Islands
J F **M A M** J J A S O N D

Iris attica
Nr. Balikesir, NW Anatolia
Dist: NW Anatolia
J F M **A M** J J A S O N D

Iridaceae: *Iris*

Fig 496
Iris gatesii
In cultivation in the UK
Dist: S and SE Anatolia
J F M **A M J** J A S O N D

Fig 497
Iris kirkwoodii
Nr Antakya, S Anatolia
Dist: S Anatolia
J F M **A M J** J A S O N D

Fig 498
Iris kirkwoodii
Nr Antakya, S Anatolia
Dist: S Anatolia
J F M **A M J** J A S O N D

Fig 499
Iris paradoxa f. choschab
Van, SE Anatolia
Dist: E Anatolia, NW Iran
J F M **A M J** J A S O N D

Iridaceae: *Iris*

Iris iberica* ssp. *elegantissima
Muradiye, E Anatolia
Dist: E Anatolia, NW Iran
J F M **A M J** J A S O N D

Iris iberica* ssp. *elegantissima
Doğubayazit, E Anatolia
Dist: E Anatolia, NW Iran
J F M **A M J** J A S O N D

Iris iberica* ssp. *lycotis
Nr. Semirom, W Iran
Dist: SE Anatolia, W Iran
J F M **A M J** J A S O N D

Iris iberica* ssp. *lycotis
Nr. Semirom, W Iran
Dist: SE Anatolia, W Iran
J F M **A M J** J A S O N D

Iridaceae: *Iris*

Iris iberica* ssp. *elegantissima
Nr. Van, SE Anatolia
Dist: E Anatolia, NW Iran
J F M **A M J** J A S O N D

Iris sari
Çatak Valley, SE Anatolia
Dist: Inner and S Anatolia
J F M **A M J** J A S O N D

Iris sari
Çatak Valley, SE Anatolia
Dist: Inner and S Anatolia
J F M **A M J** J A S O N D

Iris sari
Çatak Valley, SE Anatolia
Dist: Inner and S Anatolia
J F M **A M J** J A S O N D

Iridaceae: *Iris*

Fig 508

Iris meda
Miyan Dasht, NW Iran
Dist; NW Iran
J F **M A M** J J A S O N D

Fig 509

Iris meda
Miyan Dasht, NW Iran
Dist; NW Iran
J F **M A M** J J A S O N D

Fig 510

Iris meda
Miyan Dasht, NW Iran
Dist; NW Iran
J F **M A M** J J A S O N D

Fig 511

Iris meda
Miyan Dasht, NW Iran
Dist; NW Iran
J F **M A M** J J A S O N D

Iridaceae: *Iris*

***Iris meda* hybrids**
Nr. Salehebad, NW Iran
Dist: NW Iran
J F M A **M** J J A S O N D

***Iris meda* hybrids**
Nr. Salehebad, NW Iran
Dist: NW Iran
J F M A **M** J J A S O N D

***Iris meda* hybrids**
Nr. Salehebad, NW Iran
Dist: NW Iran
J F M A **M** J J A S O N D

***Iris meda* hybrids**
Nr. Salehebad, NW Iran
Dist: NW Iran
J F M A **M** J J A S O N D

Iridaceae: *Iris*

Iris barnumae f. barnumae
Nr. Van, SE Anatolia
Dist: SE Anatolia, NW Iran
J F M A **M J** J A S O N D

Iris barnumae f. protonyma
Nr. Bonab, NW Iran
Dist: NW Iran
J F M A **M J** J A S O N D

Iris barnumae f. urmiensis
Nr. Salmar, NW Iran
Dist: SE Anatolia, NW Iran
J F M A **M J** J A S O N D

Iris barnumae f. urmiensis
Nr. Başkale, SE Anatolia
Dist: SE Anatolia, NW Iran
J F M A **M J** J A S O N D

Iridaceae: *Iris*

Fig 520

Fig 521

Iris barnumae* ssp. *demawendica
Kandova Pass, NW Iran
Dist: N and C Iran
J F M A **M J J** A S O N D

Iris acutiloba* ssp. *lineolata
Kuh-e-Sabalan, NW Iran
Dist: N, W and S Iran
J F M **A M** J J A S O N D

Fig 522

Fig 523

Iris acutiloba* ssp. *lineolata
Nr. Zanjan, N Iran
Dist: N, W and S Iran
J F M **A M** J J A S O N D

Iris acutiloba* ssp. *lineolata
Nr. Zanjan, N Iran
Dist: N, W and S Iran
J F M **A M** J J A S O N D

Iridaceae: *Iris*

Iris reticulata v. *reticulata*
Nr. Erzurum, E Anatolia
Dist: E Anatolia, W Iran
J F **M A M J** J A S O N D

Fig 524

Fig 525

Iris reticulata v. *reticulata*
Olang, N Iran
Dist: E Anatolia, W Iran
J F **M A M J** J A S O N D

Fig 526

Iris reticulata v. *bakeriana*
In cultivation in the UK
Dist: E Anatolia, W Iran
J F **M A M J** J A S O N D

Fig 527

Iris reticulata v. *hyrcana*
Kuh-e-Sabalan, NW Iran
Dist: NW Iran
J F **M A M J** J A S O N D

Fig 528

Iris reticulata v. *hyrcana*
Asalem Pass, NW Iran
Dist: NW Iran
J F **M A M J** J A S O N D

Iridaceae: *Iris*

Iris histrioides
Amasya, N Anatolia
Dist: N Anatolia
J F **M A** M J J A S O N D

Iris histrio
Nr. Gaziantep, S Anatolia
Dist: S Anatolia
J F M A M J J A S O N D

Iris danfordiae
Sariçiçek Dağ, Anatolia
Dist: N, C and S Anatolia
J F **M A** M J J A S O N D

Iris pamphylica
Nr. Akseki, S Anatolia
Dist: S Anatolia
J F M **A M** J J A S O N D

Iris danfordiae
Arslanköy, C Anatolia
Dist: N, C and S Anatolia
J F **M A** M J J A S O N D

Iridaceae: *Iris*

Iris aucheri
Nr. Antakya, S Anatolia
Dist: S and E Anatolia, NW Iran
J **F M A** M J J A S O N D

Iris caucasica ssp. turcica
Karabet Pass, SE Anatolia
Dist: Inner Anatolia
J F M A M **J** J A S O N D

Iris caucasica ssp. caucasica
Çam Pass, NE Anatolia
Dist: NE Anatolia
J F M A M **J** J A S O N D

Iris pseudocaucasica
Nr. Hoşap, SE Anatolia
Dist: SE Anatolia, N and NW Iran
J F **M A M** J J A S O N D

Iridaceae: *Iris*

Iris kopetdagensis
Golestan, NE Iran
Dist: NE Iran
J F **M A M** J J A S O N D

Iris fosteriana
Golestan, NE Iran
Dist: N and NE Iran
J F **M A** M J J A S O N D

Iris stenophylla
Nr. Ibradi, S Anatolia
Dist: S Anatolia
J F **M A** M J J A S O N D

Iris stenophylla
Nr. Kayseri, C Anatolia
Dist: S Anatolia
J F **M A** M J J A S O N D

Iridaceae: *Iris*

Iris stenophylla
Camliyayla, S Anatolia
Dist: S Anatolia
J F **M A** M J J A S O N D

Iris galatica
Erzincan, C Anatolia
Dist: C Anatolia
J F **M A** M J J A S O N D

Iris galatica
Nr. Şiran, C Anatolia
Dist: C Anatolia
J F **M A** M J J A S O N D

Iris persica
Hop Pass, S Anatolia
Dist: S and SE Anatolia
J **F M A** M J J A S O N D

Iris persica
Ahir Dağ, Maraş, S Anatolia
Dist: S and SE Anatolia
J F **M A** M J J A S O N D

Iris persica
Nr. Gaziantep, S Anatolia
Dist: S and SE Anatolia
J **F M A** M J J A S O N D

Iridaceae: Hermodactylus/Gynandriris

Hermodactylus

This genus has only a single species with a tuberous rootstock and Iris-like flowers.

Hermodactylus tuberosus (Fig. 548)
This species is widespread in the Mediterranean region but in this area is only found in W Anatolia and the Islands, particularly Chios. The flowers are yellow-green with velvety black falls. It grows in grassy and rocky habitats.

Gynandriris

This is another Iris-related genus with a single member in the area.

Gynandriris sisyrinchium (Fig. 549)
This is another common Mediterranean species which reaches its eastern limit in western Turkey. It has small blue Iris-like flowers which only open in the afternoons. It has a cormous root and 2 long, narrow leaves. The flowers are borne in groups of 1-3 and each only lasts for a few hours. It grows in macchie, hills and flats in Turkey-in-Europe, Outer Anatolia and the Islands.

Fig 548
Hermodactylus tuberosus
Island of Chios
Dist: W Anatolia, Islands
J F **M A M** J J A S O N D

Fig 549
Gynandriris sisyrinchium
Nr. Antalya, S Anatolia
Dist: Turkey-in-Europe, Outer Anatolia, Islands
J **F M A M** J J A S O N D

Iridaceae: *Crocus*

Crocus

This is a very large and difficult genus in this area, and in Turkey alone there are more than 30 species, and about 8 species in Iran. Many of these have several recognised subspecies, so this increases the overall number to be considered.

Important characteristics botanically are the corm tunic, the number and width of the leaves, the flower colour detail, the colour of the anthers and the extent of division of the style.

Autumn-flowering Species

Crocus scharojanii ssp. lazicus (Figs. 550, 551)
This is the only autumn-flowering *Crocus* with wholly yellow or orange flowers. It is found in damp alpine pastures, often near streams, at 2,500-3,500m in NE Anatolia.

Crocus vallicola (Figs. 552, 553)
The similar, white-flowered, *C. vallicola* also comes from alpine meadows in NE Anatolia, and hybrids between them with pale yellow flowers have been reported. The style divides into 3 short, pale yellow, feathery branches. The perianth segments of the flower in **Fig. 553** have not separated completely, perhaps providing protection for the flower in adverse conditions.

Crocus kotschyanus (Figs. 554–556)
This species has white or lilac flowers with a whitish or yellowish throat, and the base of the tepals has two yellow spots. The anthers are white or cream and the style is divided into 3 or more slender, yellow branches.

Four subspecies are recognised, ***ssp. suworowianus*** (**Fig. 554**) with white flowers, found in C and N Anatolia, ***ssp. kotschyanus*** (**Fig. 555**) with lilac flowers from S Anatolia, ***ssp. cappadocicus*** (**Fig. 556**), with lilac flowers having a glabrous throat, from Inner Anatolia, and ***ssp. hakkariensis*** *(not illustrated)* with lilac flowers from SE Anatolia.

Crocus karduchorum (Fig. 557)
This is a lilac-blue flowered species with a white throat, and it comes from oak scrub at about 2,000m in the Lake Van area of SE Anatolia. The style divides into 20 or more whitish branches.

Crocus gilanicus (Fig. 558)
This local species from NW Iran is most similar to forms of *C. kotschyanus*. It has white flowers often with purple veins, but the throat is without yellow blotches. It grows in beech forests and mountain meadows at 1,500-2,500m.

Crocus pallasii (Figs. 559–562)
This is a species with lilac-blue to reddish-purple flowers often with darker veins. The style divides into 3 red or orange branches. It grows on stony mountainsides and in open woods and scrub at altitudes of up to 2,000m.

It again has four recognised subspecies, ***ssp. pallasii*** (**Figs. 559, 560**) from Turkey-in-Europe, N, W, C and S Anatolia with pale to deep lilac flowers, the similar ***ssp. turcicus*** (not illustrated) from SE Anatolia, particularly Gaziantep and Diyarbakir provinces, ***ssp. dispathaceus*** (**Fig. 562**) with deep reddish-purple flowers from the Içel and Konya areas, and lilac-blue ***ssp. haussknechtii*** (**Fig. 561**) from dry fields in W Iran.

Crocus sativus (Fig. 563)
This is the *Crocus* from which saffron is obtained, and it is now an essentially cultivated rather than wild species. Often considered to be a selected form of *C. cartwrightianus* (**Fig. 564**) from Crete and Greece, *C. sativus* has deep, lilac-purple flowers with very prominent styles which divide into 3 long, red branches.

Crocus asumaniae (Fig. 565)
This is a species which is also closely related to *C. cartwrightianus* and has only been found in the Akseki area of S Anatolia. It has white to pale lilac flowers with darker veins at the base and a style divided into 3 long, orange-red branches.

Crocus mathewii (Figs. 566, 567)
This very attractive species comes from the Lycian Taurus area west of Antalya, and is usually white-flowered with a deep violet throat. The anthers are yellow and the 3-branched style is orange. The amount of purple on the throat is variable, and a particularly good form is shown in **Fig. 566**.

Crocus cancellatus (Figs. 568–573)
This is a variable *Crocus* with five recognised subspecies. It has lilac-blue or white flowers which are usually veined or darker at the base, and is found in rocky places and macchie. The most distinctive subspecies is ***ssp. pamphylicus*** (**Fig. 568**) which has flowers with white anthers and a deep yellow or orange throat to the corolla, and this is found in the Central Taurus Mountains. The other subspecies have yellow anthers. The ***ssp. cancellatus*** (not illustrated) is found in the Taurus and Amanus Mountains of S Anatolia, ***ssp. mazziaricus*** (**Figs. 569, 570**) in NW, W and C Anatolia and the Islands, ***ssp. lycius*** (**Figs. 571, 572**) in the Lycia region of S Anatolia and ***ssp. damascenus*** (**Fig. 573**) in

the Amanus area and in Inner Anatolia. This species also occurs in W Iran.

Crocus speciosus (Figs. 574,575)
This is a species which is very well-known to gardeners, having large, lilac flowers with distinct, darker veins, and a bright orange, much-branched style. In Turkey it is found mainly in N and C Anatolia growing in mountain meadows and open woodland, and it is also found in N Iran. It is variable over its wide distribution area and three subspecies have been identified. The typical form, **ssp. speciosus** has large flowers, but *ssp. ilgazensis* from N Anatolia (Çankiri and Amasya) has smaller flowers with a style exceeded by the anthers. The third subspecies, *ssp. xantholaimos*, also from N Anatolia (Sinop), has a flower with a deep yellow throat.

Crocus pulchellus (Fig. 576)
This is similar to *C. speciosus* but the throat of the flower is strongly yellow. The filaments are densely pubescent and the anthers white rather than yellow. It occurs in open oak and pinewoods in NW Turkey and the Islands.

Crocus tournefortii (Fig. 577)
This lilac-flowered species is found on the island of Rhodes and is distinguished by the leaves being present at the time of flowering. It grows in open stony ground and scrub.

Crocus caspius (Fig. 578)
This is a species with white to purplish-violet flowers with a deep yellow throat. The anthers are yellow and the 3-branched style is orange. It comes from woods and grassy scrub in the Caspian region and the Alborz foothills in N Iran.

Crocus wattiorum (Fig. 579)
This was originally named as a subspecies of *C. biflorus* but is now accepted as a separate species. It is very distinct because it is autumn-flowering and has lilac-blue flowers with blackish anthers and very long, red style branches. It has been found on Tahtali Dağ in the Antalya area of S. Anatolia growing in crevices in limestone rocks.

Crocus nerimaniae (Fig. 580)
This recently named species is similar to *C. wattiorum*. It is leafless at flowering time and has pale lilac flowers with a contrasting dark violet stain at the base and blackish-violet anthers. It is found in rock crevices and on open hillsides in the Milas area of SW Anatolia.

Spring-flowering Species.
Flowers wholly yellow or orange. Style divided into at least 6 branches.

Crocus olivieri (Figs. 581–583)
This species has 1-4, spreading or falcate leaves and yellow to orange-yellow flowers, and grows on open, rocky hillsides and in macchie. Three subspecies are recognised, one of which, **ssp. istanbulensis**, occurs very locally in Istanbul. The **ssp. olivieri** (Figs. 581, 582) has flowers with styles divided into 6 branches, and without any markings on the outside of the tepals. It is found in Turkey-in-Europe, N, W, C and S Anatolia and the Islands. The **ssp. balansae** (Fig. 583) has brown stripes or markings on the outside of the flower and the style is divided into 12-15 branches. It grows in W Anatolia and the Islands.

Crocus graveolens (Fig. 584)
This is another species with bright, orange-yellow flowers, which are usually striped or suffused with brown on the outside. The style is divided into many, very fine, yellow branches. The plant has 5-8 grey-green leaves and grows on stony hillsides amongst open macchie or scrub in S Anatolia.

Crocus vitellinus (Fig. 585)
This is a similar species from the Hatay region of S Anatolia, but it has 2-4 shiny green leaves and more rounded tepals. It grows in grassy places in the mountains or in light woodland.

Flowers wholly yellow or orange. Style divided into 3 branches.

Crocus flavus (Fig. 586)
This *Crocus* has 4-8 erect leaves and bright yellow to orange-yellow flowers, and is found in woods and scrub in Turkey-in-Europe, and N and W Anatolia. In some forms from W Turkey (*ssp. dissectus*) the style can be 6-15 branched.

Crocus chrysanthus (Figs. 587–589)
This widespread yellow to orange-flowered species occurs throughout Anatolia except for the east, and in Turkey-in-Europe and the Islands. It grows on open, grassy hillsides and in scrub, and the flowers are often bronze or purplish on the outside. The style is 3-branched and the anthers are normally yellow, but forms with black anthers are occasionally found (Fig. 589).

It hybridises with closely related species, particularly forms of the *C. biflorus* group (Figs. 590, 591).

Crocus danfordiae (Figs. 592,593)
This species is closely related to *C. chrysanthus*, but is recognised by its smaller pale yellow, lilac-blue or white flowers, which are usually speckled outside with grey or purple. It grows on open hillsides in C and S Anatolia.

Iridaceae: *Crocus*

Crocus almehensis (Fig. 594)
This yellow-flowered species is also close to *C. chrysanthus*, but it comes from the Gorgan area of NE Iran. It has orange-yellow flowers which are often striped or suffused with bronze on the outside, and it has 3-4 relatively broad (3-5mm) leaves. It grows in steppe and mountain pastures near melting snow.

Crocus gargaricus (Fig. 595,596)
This is a yellow or orange-flowered *Crocus* from damp pastures in NW Anatolia (*ssp. herbertii*), and drier places in SW Anatolia (*ssp. gargaricus*). It has 3-4 narrow leaves and the style is divided into 3 feathery branches.

Crocus ancyrensis (Fig. 597)
This bright yellow species has flowers that are often stained purplish at the base and on the outside of the perianth tube. It has yellow anthers and the style is divided into 3 orange branches. It grows in open rocky places in N and C Anatolia.

Crocus sieheanus (Fig. 598)
This is another yellow or orange *Crocus* from open hillsides and pinewoods in S and C Anatolia. It is closely related to *C. ancyrensis* but is distinguished by differences in the corm tunic.

Flowers white, usually with a yellow throat. Style divided into 6 or more branches.

Crocus fleischeri (Fig. 599)
This *Crocus* has white flowers which are yellow at the base and often stained purple at the base and on the perianth tube. The anthers are yellow and the style is divided into at least 6 orange to scarlet branches. It grows on open hillsides or in oak scrub in S and W Anatolia and on the Islands.

Crocus candidus (Fig. 600)
This species has 1-2 leaves but often flowers with only one leaf present. Its white flowers distinguish it from the closely related *C. olivieri*. It grows in macchie and phrygana in NW Anatolia and possibly on the island of Lesbos.

Crocus antalyensis (Fig. 601)
This species has 3-8 leaves and white or pale lilac-blue flowers with a yellow throat. The anthers are pale yellow and the style is divided into 6-12 yellow or orange branches. It occurs in open oak woodland or scrub in W Anatolia.

Flowers white, usually with a yellow throat. Style divided into 3 branches.

Crocus reticulatus (Figs. 602,603)
This species has white or lilac-blue flowers with the outer tepals strongly striped with purple or violet. It grows in open rocky places or pinewoods, and there are two subspecies, **ssp. reticulatus** (Fig. 603) from C and S Anatolia, and **ssp. hittiticus** (Fig. 602) from the Içel area of S Anatolia. The distinguishing feature is the colour of the anthers, yellow in *ssp. reticulatus* and blackish in *ssp. hittiticus*.

Crocus pestalozzae (Figs. 604,605)
This is a yellow-throated, white or lilac-blue flowered *Crocus* from NW Turkey, which is closely related to *C. biflorus*. It is distinguished by its green, sheathing leaves, and the black stain at the base of the filaments. It is a low altitude species growing in short turf.

Crocus biflorus (Figs. 606–617)
This species is by far the most difficult in the genus as it is widespread and variable with at least 10 subspecies recognised in Turkey alone. A few forms are also present in N and W Iran. It grows on open rocky slopes, in scrub or in alpine turf at up to 3,000m.

One of the most restricted subspecies in this region is **ssp. biflorus** itself (Fig. 606), which is only found in the Istanbul area and on the island of Rhodes. It is distinguished by the leaves which have no prominent ribs in the grooves on their lower surface; all other forms have at least one prominent rib. The flowers are white and the outside is purple-striped.

The next group, **ssp. tauri** (Figs. 607, 608) and **ssp. pulchricolor** (Figs. 609–611) have lilac to blue flowers which do not have very obvious stripes on the outside. The anthers are yellow. The *ssp. tauri* is a mountain plant from S and Inner Anatolia, and it has 4-9 leaves which are broader than with *ssp. pulchricolor*. The latter comes from NW Anatolia and has 3-4, narrow leaves up to 1mm broad.

The other subspecies are all strongly striped on the outside and most have at least 3 stripes, but **ssp. artvinensis** (not illustrated) is distinct in only having one. The anthers of this form are yellow and it is found in the Çoruh Valley area of NE Anatolia.

The **ssp. crewei** (Fig. 612) comes from SW Anatolia, and is distinguished by its blackish anthers. It has 2-3, relatively wide leaves, and grows on mountains in the Denizli and Isparta Provinces.

The other subspecies generally have 4-8 narrow leaves (up to 1mm). The **ssp. nubigena** (Fig. 613) is recognised by the dense, hair-like projections on its style branches. It has blackish-maroon anthers and is found in W and SW Anatolia and on the Islands.

The next subspecies is **ssp. punctatus** (Fig. 614) which is characterised by the finely-speckled outside to the corolla, rather than it being striped. It grows in S Anatolia in the Isparta and Burdur Provinces.

The **ssp. pseudonubigena** (Fig. 615) form has flowers which are clove-scented and have blackish anthers. It grows in much drier areas amongst oak scrub in SE Anatolia from Gaziantep to Bitlis.

The **ssp. adamii** (not illustrated), with the rare *ssp. biflorus*, is the only form in Turkey-in-Europe. It has lilac flowers with 3-5 strong stripes on the outside and yellow anthers. It also occurs in NE Iran.

The **ssp. isauricus** (Figs. 616, 617) is quite widespread in S Anatolia occurring in provinces from Muğla to İçel. It has 4-7 narrow, grey-green leaves, and white or lilac flowers which are striped or speckled on the outside with purple or grey-purple. It grows on open limestone hillsides or in open coniferous woodland at 1,000-2,000m.

Flowers lilac or blue with or without a yellow throat. Style usually 3-branched.

(Note that colour forms of *C. antalyensis, C. reticulatus, C. pestalozzae, C. danfordiae* and *C. biflorus* come under this grouping also)

Crocus baytopiorum (Fig. 618)
This species is characterised by its pale, clear blue flowers, which have fine veins of a darker colour. The style is yellow and the plant is only known from a few localities in the Denizli and Antalya regions of W and SW Anatolia.

Crocus abantensis (Fig. 619)
This *Crocus* is only known from the Lake Abant area of NW Turkey. It has mid- to deep-blue flowers with a yellow throat, and the style is divided into 3 slender, orange branches. It has 5-10 narrow leaves and grows amongst pines and junipers.

Crocus leichtlinii (Fig. 620)
This species was originally named as a subspecies of *C. biflorus*, but was recognised as a separate species in the 1920's. It has heather-scented, pale blue flowers, which are stained darker slatey-blue on the outside, and they have a deep yellow throat. It is found, often on volcanic soils, in SE Anatolia.

Crocus kerndorffiorum (Fig. 621)
This is a recently named *Crocus* from the eastern Taurus Mountains of S Anatolia. It is related to *C. leichtlinii* and has lilac flowers with violet veining or feathering. The anthers are bluish-green and the red style is 3-branched.

Crocus adanensis (Fig. 622)
This is a rare species from the Adana area of S Anatolia, and it grows in mixed woodland at about 1,000m. It has pale, lilac-blue flowers with a large white or creamy zone in the centre. *Crocus paschei* may be synonymous with this.

Crocus aerius (Figs. 623,624)
This is a mountain species occurring at over 2,000m in damp turf at the edge of snow patches in NE Anatolia (Trabzon region). It has deep blue flowers with darker veins and a darker centre, and it has a pale yellow throat.

Crocus michelsonii (Fig. 625)
This is the only member of the Orientales section of *Crocus* present in our area. It is a beautiful species with white flowers heavily suffused or speckled on the outside with lilac-blue. The style is divided into three whitish branches. It grows on open stony hills or in *Artemesia* steppe in the Kopet Dağ range of NE Iran.

Fig 550
Crocus scharojanii ssp. lazicus
Nr. Uzungöl, NE Anatolia
Dist: NE Anatolia
J F M A M J **J A S O** N D

Fig 551
Crocus scharojanii ssp. lazicus
In cultivation in the UK
Dist: NE Anatolia
J F M A M J **J A S O** N D

Iridaceae: *Crocus*

Crocus vallicola
Nr. Uzungöl, NE Anatolia
Dist: NE Anatolia
J F M A M J J **A S O** N D

Crocus vallicola
Nr. Uzungöl, NE Anatolia
Dist: NE Anatolia
J F M A M J J **A S O** N D

Crocus kotschyanus ssp. suworowianus
From Erzurum, C Anatolia
Dist: C and N Anatolia
J F M A M J J A **S O N** D

Crocus kotschyanus ssp. kotschyanus
In cultivation in the UK
Dist: S Anatolia
J F M A M J J A **S O** N D

Iridaceae: *Crocus*

Fig 556
Crocus kotschyanus* ssp. *cappadocicus
In cultivation in the UK
Dist: Inner Anatolia
J F M A M J J A **S O N** D

Fig 557
Crocus karduchorum
South of Lake Van, SE Anatolia
Dist: SE Anatolia
J F M A M J J A **S O N** D

Fig 558
Crocus gilanicus
From Gilan, NW Iran
Dist: NW Iran
J F M A M J J A **S O N** D

Fig 559
Crocus pallasii* ssp. *pallasii
In cultivation in the UK
Dist: Turkey-in-Europe, N, W, C and S Anatolia
J F M A M J J A **S O N** D

Iridaceae: *Crocus*

Fig 560
Crocus pallasii* ssp. *pallasii (white form)
From Antalya, S Anatolia
Dist: Turkey-in-Europe, N, W, C and S Anatolia
J F M A M J J A S **O N D**

Fig 561
Crocus pallasii* ssp. *haussknechtii
From Zagros Mountains, W Iran
Dist: W Iran
J F M A M J J A S **O N D**

Fig 562
Crocus pallasii* ssp. *dispathaceus
From Içel, S Anatolia
Dist: S Anatolia
J F M A M J J A **S O N D**

Fig 563
Crocus sativus
Safranbolu, N Anatolia
Dist: Cultivated locally
J F M A M J J A **S O N D**

Iridaceae: *Crocus*

Fig 564
Crocus cartwrightianus
Crete
Dist: Greece and Islands
J F M A M J J A **S O N** D

Fig 565
Crocus asumaniae
In cultivation in the UK
Dist: SW Anatolia
J F M A M J J A S **O N** D

Fig 566
Crocus mathewii
From near Antalya, S Anatolia
Dist: S Anatolia (Lycian Taurus)
J F M A M J J A S **O N** D

Fig 567
Crocus mathewii (white form)
Near Antalya, S Anatolia
Dist: S Anatolia (Lycian Taurus)
J F M A M J J A S **O N** D

Fig 568
Crocus cancellatus* ssp. *pamphylicus
From near Akseki, S Anatolia
Dist: S Anatolia
J F M A M J J A **S O N** D

215

Iridaceae: *Crocus*

Crocus cancellatus* ssp. *mazziaricus
Nr. Muğla, SW Anatolia
Dist: NW, W and C Anatolia, Islands
J F M A M J J A **S O N** D

Crocus cancellatus* ssp. *mazziaricus
Nr. Muğla, SW Anatolia
Dist: NW, W and C Anatolia, Islands
J F M A M J J A **S O N** D

Crocus cancellatus* ssp. *lycius
Nr. Finike, S Anatolia
Dist: S Anatolia
J F M A M J J A **S O N** D

Crocus cancellatus* ssp. *lycius
Nr. Finike, S Anatolia
Dist: S Anatolia
J F M A M J J A **S O N** D

Iridaceae: *Crocus*

Crocus cancellatus* ssp. *damascenus
Nur Dağ Pass, Inner Anatolia
Dist: S and Inner Anatolia, W Iran
J F M A M J J A **S O N** D

Crocus speciosus* ssp *speciosus
Tahtali Dağ, S Anatolia
Dist: N, C and S Anatolia
J F M A M J J A S **O N** D

Crocus speciosus* ssp. *speciosus
Tahtali Dağ, S Anatolia
Dist: N, C and S Anatolia
J F M A M J J A S **O N** D

Crocus pulchellus
Çanakkale, NW Turkey
Dist: NW Turkey, Islands
J F M A M J J A S **O N** D

Iridaceae: *Crocus*

Crocus tournefortii
From Island of Rhodes
Dist: Islands
J F M A M J J A **S O N D**

Crocus caspius
From Alborz Mts, N Iran
Dist: N Iran
J F M A M J J A **S O N D**

Crocus wattiorum
Nr. Antalya, S Anatolia
Dist: S Anatolia (Antalya)
J F M A M J J A S **O N D**

Crocus nerimaniae
From Milas, Aydın, SW Anatolia
Dist: SW Anatolia (Aydın and Muğla)
J F M A M J J A S **O N D**

Crocus olivieri* ssp. *olivieri
Lake Abant, Bolu, N Anatolia
Dist: Turkey-in-Europe, Anatolia except east, Islands
J **F M A M** J J A S O N D

Crocus olivieri* ssp. *olivieri
Lake Abant, Bolu, N Anatolia
Dist: Turkey-in-Europe, Anatolia except east, Islands
J **F M A M** J J A S O N D

Iridaceae: *Crocus*

Crocus olivieri* ssp. *balansae
In cultivation in the UK
Dist: W Antolia, Islands
J F M A M J J A S O N D

Crocus graveolens
From Ermenek, S Anatolia
Dist: S Anatolia
J F M A M J J A S O N D

Crocus vitellinus
In cultivation in the UK
Dist: S Anatolia (Hatay)
J F M A M J J A S O N D

Crocus flavus
From Ulu Dağ, Bursa, NW Anatolia
Dist: Turkey-in-Europe, N and W Anatolia
J F M A M J J A S O N D

Crocus chrysanthus
Gembos Yayla, S Anatolia
Dist: Turkey-in-Europe, Anatolia except east, Islands
J F M A M J J A S O N D

Crocus chrysanthus
Gembos Yayla, S Anatolia
Dist: Turkey-in-Europe, Anatolia except east, Islands
J F M A M J J A S O N D

Iridaceae: *Crocus*

Crocus chrysanthus
From Honaz Dağ, SW Anatolia
Dist: Turkey-in-Europe, Anatolia except east, Islands
J **F M A** M J J A S O N D

Crocus chrysanthus x C. biflorus ssp. isauricus
Nr. Ibradi, S Anatolia

Crocus chrysanthus x C. biflorus ssp. pulchricolor
Ulu Dağ, Bursa, N Anatolia

Crocus danfordiae
From Ak Dağ, C Anatolia
Dist: C and S Anatolia
J **F M A** M J J A S O N D

Crocus danfordiae
From Ak Dağ, C Anatolia
Dist: C and S Anatolia
J **F M A** M J J A S O N D

Iridaceae: Crocus

Crocus almehensis
Golestan, NE Iran
Dist: NE Iran
J F M **A M** J J A S O N D

Crocus gargaricus ssp. herbertii
Ulu Dağ, Bursa, NW Anatolia
Dist: NW Anatolia
J F M **A M** J J A S O N D

Crocus gargaricus ssp. herbertii
Ulu Dağ, Bursa, NW Anatolia
Dist: NW Anatolia
J F M **A M** J J A S O N D

Crocus ancyrensis
Abant, Bolu, N Anatolia
Dist: N and C Anatolia
J **F M A M** J J A S O N D

Crocus sieheanus
In cultivation in the UK
Dist: S and C Anatolia
J F M **A M** J J A S O N D

Iridaceae: *Crocus*

Crocus fleischeri
Nr. Muğla, SW Anatolia
Dist: S and W Anatolia, Islands
J F M A M J J A S O N D

Crocus candidus
In cultivation in the UK
Dist: NW Anatolia
J F M A M J J A S O N D

Crocus antalyensis
In cultivation in the UK
Dist: W Anatolia
J F M A M J J A S O N D

Crocus reticulatus ssp. hittiticus
Silifke, S Anatolia
Dist: S Anatolia (Içel)
J F M A M J J A S O N D

Crocus reticulatus ssp. reticulatus
Arslanköy, C Anatolia
Dist: C and S Anatolia
J F M A M J J A S O N D

Iridaceae: *Crocus*

Crocus pestalozzae
In cultivation in the UK
Dist: NW Turkey
J F M A M J J A S O N D

Crocus pestalozzae v. alba
From Çamlica, NW Turkey
Dist: NW Turkey
J F M A M J J A S O N D

Crocus biflorus ssp. biflorus
From Colosimi, Italy
Dist: NW Turkey (Istanbul), Rhodes
J F M A M J J A S O N D

Crocus biflorus ssp. tauri
Kirecli Pass, E Anatolia
Dist: S and Inner Anatolia
J F M A M J J A S O N D

Crocus biflorus ssp. tauri
Nr. Erzurum, E Anatolia
Dist: S and Inner Anatolia
J F M A M J J A S O N D

Iridaceae: *Crocus*

Crocus biflorus ssp. pulchricolor
Ulu Dağ, Bursa, NW Anatolia
Dist: NW Anatolia
J F **M A M J** J A S O N D

Crocus biflorus ssp. pulchricolor
Ulu Dağ, Bursa, NW Anatolia
Dist: NW Anatolia
J F **M A M J** J A S O N D

Crocus biflorus ssp. pulchricolor
Ulu Dağ, Bursa, NW Anatolia
Dist: NW Anatolia
J F **M A M J** J A S O N D

Crocus biflorus ssp. crewei
Honaz Dağ, SW Anatolia
Dist: SW Anatolia
J F **M A M J** J A S O N D

Crocus biflorus ssp. nubigena
From Ibradi, S Anatolia
Dist: W and SW Anatolia, Islands
J **F M** A M J J A S O N D

Iridaceae: *Crocus*

Crocus biflorus* ssp. *punctatus
In cultivation in the UK
Dist: S Anatolia (Isparta and Burdur)
J **F M A** M J J A S O N D

Crocus biflorus* ssp. *pseudonubigena
From Gaziantep, S Anatolia
Dist: SE Anatolia
J **F M A** M J J A S O N D

Crocus biflorus* ssp. *isauricus
Nr. Ibradi, S Anatolia
Dist: S Anatolia
J F **M A** M J J A S O N D

Crocus biflorus* ssp. *isauricus
Nr. Ibradi, S Anatolia
Dist: S Anatolia
J F **M A** M J J A S O N D

Iridaceae: *Crocus*

Crocus baytopiorum
Denizli, SW Anatolia
Dist: S and SW Anatolia, Islands
J F **M A M** J J A S O N D

Crocus abantensis
Lake Abant, Bolu, NW Anatolia
Dist: NW Anatolia
J F M **A M** J J A S O N D

Crocus leichtlinii
In cultivation in the UK
Dist: SE Anatolia
J F **M A M** J J A S O N D

Crocus kerndorffiorum
From E Taurus, S Anatolia
Dist: S Anatolia
J F **M A M** J J A S O N D

Iridaceae: *Crocus*

Fig 622
Crocus adanensis
From Adana, S Anatolia
Dist: S Anatolia (N Amanus)
J F **M A** M J J A S O N D

Fig 623
Crocus aerius
Zigana Pass, NE Anatolia
Dist: NE Anatolia
J F M **A M** J J A S O N D

Fig 624
Crocus aerius
Zigana Pass, NE Anatolia
Dist: NE Anatolia
J F M **A M** J J A S O N D

Fig 625
Crocus michelsonii
From Kopet Dağ, NE Iran
Dist: NE Iran
J F **M A** M J J A S O N D

Iridaceae: *Romulea*

Romulea

This group of crocus-like plants occurs mainly in the Mediterranean region of Turkey. None are present in Iran. There are five species in the area which are reasonably distinct.

Romulea bulbocodium (Figs. 626–628)

This widespread Mediterranean species is found in S and SW Anatolia and the Islands, occurring in several colour forms which are given varietal status. ***R. bulbocodium* v. *bulbocodium* (Fig. 626)** has lilac or violet flowers, and **v. *leichtliniana* (Fig. 628)** has white flowers. The third form **v. *crocea*** has yellow flowers **(Fig. 627)**.

Romulea tempskyana (Fig. 629)

This is another violet-flowered species with a yellow centre, but the perianth tube is longer than with *R. bulbocodium* and the filaments are glabrous rather than hairy. It occurs in open woodland in W and S Anatolia and the Islands.

Romulea linaresii ssp. graeca (Fig. 630)

This violet-flowered *Romulea* has much smaller flowers than the previous species and the centre of the flower is violet or dark violet. It grows in macchie in W Turkey and the Islands.

Romulea ramiflora (Fig. 631)

This is a pale to deep lilac-blue flowered species with a yellow throat which grows in sandy coastal situations in W Turkey and the Islands, and in the Amanus region of S Anatolia.

Romulea columnae (Fig. 632)

This species has small pale lilac to whitish flowers and is another species growing at close to sea level in open, grassy places or damp river banks. It is found in W Turkey, S Anatolia and the Islands.

Fig 626

Romulea bulbocodium* ssp. *bulbocodium
Island of Lesbos
Dist: W and S Anatolia, Islands
J **F M A M** J A S O N D

Fig 627

Romulea bulbocodium* ssp. *crocea
Nr. Akseki, S Anatolia
Dist: S and SW Anatolia
J **F M A M** J A S O N D

Iridaceae: *Romulea*

Romulea bulbocodium* ssp. *leichtliniana
Island of Chios
Dist: S Anatolia and Islands
J F **M A M** J J A S O N D

Romulea tempskyana
Cyprus
Dist: W and S Anatolia, Islands
J F M A M J J A S O N D

Romulea linaresii* ssp. *graeca
Island of Chios
Dist: W Turkey, Islands
J F **M A M** J J A S O N D

Romulea ramiflora
Island of Chios
Dist: W Turkey, S Anatolia, Islands
J F **M A M** J J A S O N D

Romulea columnae
Devon, England
Dist: W Turkey, S Anatolis, Islands
J F M A M J J A S O N D

Iridaceae: Gladiolus

Gladiolus

This is another relatively small genus in this area, the bulk of the species, as with *Romulea*, coming from South Africa. However many species are very colourful and are present in large numbers. Factors that are important in identification are leaf number, width and vein arrangement, and the relative anther and filament length.

Plants with 3-5 Leaves with Irregularly-spaced Veins. Flowers Shades of Pink

Gladiolus italicus (Figs. 633, 634)
This is the most common and widespread Mediterranean species. It is found in Turkey-in-Europe, Outer Anatolia and the Islands, and is widespread in Iran, growing generally in cultivated fields and other disturbed areas. It has a lax, 6-12 flowered spike of pink or magenta flowers with anthers longer than the filaments. The leaves are 8-12mm broad.

Gladiolus antakiensis (Fig. 635)
This is a very similar species to *G. italicus* but it has narrower leaves (up to 8mm) and is only found in the Amanus area of S Anatolia and around Mardin in the SE.

Gladiolus illyricus (Fig. 636)
This is generally a smaller *Gladiolus* which grows on rocky slopes and coastal phrygana in W Anatolia and the Islands. The anthers are shorter than the filaments and it has a spike of 3-10 deep pink flowers.

Gladiolus anatolicus (not illustrated)
This is another species from S and SW Anatolia and the Islands, and it grows in macchie on limestone soils. It has 3-4 purple flowers and a short stem (up to 40cm). It is similar to **G. triphyllus** from Cyprus **(Fig. 641)**. A similar species, *G. humilis*, occurs in the Adiyaman area of SE Anatolia, where it is a mountain plant found at 2000m on Nemrut Dağ.

Plants with 2 Leaves with Irregularly-spaced Veins

Gladiolus kotschyanus (Figs. 637–640)
This *Gladiolus*, which grows mainly in E Anatolia, is probably the species with the greatest range of flower colour. It occurs in damp fields or along rivers and often grows in very large numbers. It has 2 leaves rather than the 3-5 of the other species in this group. It is also found in NW Iran.

Plants with Leaves with Parallel Veins

Gladiolus persicus (Fig. 642)
This species has relatively small pink to purple flowers and rather greyish, glaucous leaves covered in short hairs. It grows on stony hillsides in S Iran. Related to this is the endemic Turkish species *G. micranthus*, which has narrower leaves and a lax spike of 3-4 lilac to violet-purple flowers. It grows amongst dolomitic limestone or volcanic rubble in SW Anatolia.

Gladiolus atroviolaceus (Figs. 643, 644)
This species is very distinctive and has a dense spike of 4-8 deep violet-purple flowers. It is mainly found in fallow fields and steppe in Inner and E Anatolia and is also distributed widely in W and S Iran.

The final species in this group, *G. halophyllus,* with 3-5 pink or magenta-pink flowers, is restricted to saline soils in C Anatolia.

Iridaceae: *Gladiolus*

Fig 633
Gladiolus italicus
Island of Lesbos
Dist: Turkey-in-Europe, Outer Anatolia, Islands
J **F M A M J** J A S O N D

Fig 634
Gladiolus italicus
Island of Lesbos
Dist: Turkey-in-Europe, Outer Anatolia, Islands
J **F M A M J** J A S O N D

Fig 635
Gladiolus antakiensis
Nr. Antakya, S Anatolia
Dist: S Anatolia (Amanus)
J F M A **M J** J A S O N D

Fig 636
Gladiolus illyricus
Island of Lesbos
Dist: W Anatolia, Islands
J F M **A M J** J A S O N D

Iridaceae: *Gladiolus*

Fig 637

Gladiolus kotschyanus
Karabet Pass, SE Anatolia
Dist: E Anatolia
J F M **A M J J A** S O N D

Fig 638

Gladiolus kotschyanus
Nr. Tatvan, SE Anatolia
Dist: E Anatolia
J F M **A M J J A** S O N D

Fig 639

Gladiolus kotschyanus
Nr. Artvin, NE Anatolia
Dist: E Anatolia
J F M **A M J J A** S O N D

Fig 640

Gladiolus kotschyanus
Lake Van, SE Anatolia
Dist: E Anatolia
J F M **A M J J A** S O N D

Iridaceae: *Gladiolus*

Gladiolus triphyllus
Cyprus
Dist: Cyprus
J F **M A M** J J A S O N D

Gladiolus persicus
Nr. Shiraz, SW Iran
Dist: S Iran
J F M **A** M J J A S O N D

Gladiolus atroviolaceus
Lake Van, SE Anatolia
Dist: E Anatolia
J F **M A M J** J A S O N D

Gladiolus atroviolaceus
Tortum, NE Anatolia
Dist: E Anatolia
J F **M A M J** J A S O N D

Orchidaceae:

Ophrys tenthredinifera, Island of Chios

Orchidaceae

The orchid family is strongly represented in the Mediterranean area and Turkey is no exception, though many species are reaching their eastern limit here. As a result Iran has a much smaller number of species.

This book does not illustrate some of the widely distributed species such as *Listera ovata* and *L. cordata*, *Gymnadenia conopsea*, *Platanthera bifolia*, *Coeloglossum viride*, *Anacamptis pyramidalis* and *Corallorhiza trifida* all of which occur in the area. Instead it concentrates on some of the species that are special to the region, are most noticeable or are in complicated groups such as *Ophrys* or *Dactylorhiza*. However it is the illustrations that are most important and no attempt is made to describe the species in detail.

The most recent and comprehensive study of the orchids of Turkey has been published by Kreutz (see Bibliography) and this should be consulted for the identification of the more difficult or localised species. Orchids in Iran are described in Volume 126 of Flora Iranica.

The flowers of plants within the orchid family are often spectacular but structurally they are complicated. The outer three parts, the sepals, are often prominent and highly coloured and they are all similar, but the inner three, the petals, are quite differently arranged. The upper two are often small and may come together to form a hood, as in *Orchis* or *Dactylorhiza*, or may be reduced to small appendages as in the case of *Ophrys*. However the third, central petal is exaggerated in shape, colour and markings, and this is known as the lip. It is often the most distinguishable feature of the particular species and may be the basis of the orchid's name.

Orchids generally have an association with mycorrhizal fungi in the soil, but most still need the normal green leaves to generate chlorophyll by the action of light. However some species are 'saprophytic' and this means that they are capable of obtaining their nourishment from the decaying leaves where they grow. They can then exist in very dark habitats in dense woodland where there is little or no ground cover. Typical examples are species in the genera *Neottia*, *Epipogium*, *Limodorum* and *Corallorhiza*.

Orchidaceae: *Cephalnthera/Epipactis*

Cephalanthera

Six species of *Cephalanthera* occur in Turkey, three of them familiar in Europe, *C. damasonium*, *C. longifolia*, and *C. rubra*, and the other three restricted to Turkey and the eastern Mediterranean.

Cephalanthera longifolia (Fig. 646)
This helleborine is found mainly in Outer Anatolia, the Islands and N and NW Iran. It has long, narrow leaves and a tall spike of small white flowers, and grows in open woodland in mountain regions and in meadows at the edge of the woods.

Cephalanthera damasonium (Fig. 647)
This species has a few, smaller, more oval leaves and fewer white flowers, which never open very widely. It grows in Turkey-in-Europe, N and W Anatolia and in N Iran, and is usually found in more shady places in the forests.

Cephalanthera kotschyana (Fig. 648)
This is an endemic plant of N, S and E Anatolia with a dense spike of up to 20 white flowers. These are large and they open widely, and the 3-4 spreading leaves are oval in shape. It grows in oak scrub on stony hillsides.

Cephalanthera epipactoides (Fig. 649)
This helleborine can be up to 1m tall and has a dense spike of many, rather pointed, white flowers with a short spur. The lower leaves are sheath-like and enclose the stem. It is found in macchie and oak scrub on limestone soils in Turkey-in-Europe, Outer Anatolia and on some of the Islands.

Cephalanthera kurdica (Fig. 650)
This species is found mainly in S and E Anatolia and in NW Iran. It grows in macchie and oak and pine forests on calcareous soils, and has a dense, many-flowered spike of pale to bright, rose-pink flowers which have a short spur.

Cephalanthera rubra (Fig. 651)
This familiar species usually has rather fewer, more widely-spaced flowers, which are bright rosy-pink to rosy-purple in colour, but are without a spur. It has longer leaves than *C. kurdica* and the stems are hairy in the upper part. It grows in similar habitats in N, SW and S Anatolia and in N and NW Iran.

There is an endemic species in the Caspian woodlands of N Iran, *C. caucasica*, which is closely related to *C. longifolia*, but it has numerous, broad leaves and a congested spike of white flowers.

Epipactis

This genus has always been difficult as there are several similar species and recent authors have divided it even more. About nine species have been recognised in Turkey and Iran, and these include the Turkish endemics, *Epipactis bithynica*, *E. pontica* and *E. turcica*, and the more widespread *E. condensata*, *E. helleborine*, *E. microphylla*, *E. persica* and *E. veratrifolia*. Of the latter all but *E. condensata* occur in Iran, mainly in the N and NW.

Only four species are illustrated here **E. palustris (Fig. 652)**, **E. veratrifolia (Fig. 653)**, **E. helleborine (Fig. 654)** and **E. pontica (Figs. 655, 656)**. The first two are distinctive and easily recognised, *E. palustris* growing in wet meadows in N Turkey, E Anatolia and NW Iran, and *E. veratrifolia* found on wet slopes and on riverbanks in E and S Anatolia. *E. pontica* is closely related to *E. helleborine* and is sometimes considered as a subspecies of it. It grows in N and NE Anatolia in beech forests along the Black Sea coast. *E. helleborine* is widespread in Turkey and Iran. An endemic Iranian species, *E. rechingeri*, which is related to *E. purpurata*, is found in damp beech forests in N Iran.

Orchidaceae: *Cephalanthera*

Fig 646
Cephalanthera longifolia
Nr. Akseki, S Anatolia
Dist: Outer Anatolia, Islands, N and NW Iran
J F M **A M J** J A S O N D

Fig 647
Cephalanthera damasonium
Zigana Pass, N Anatolia
Dist: N and W Anatolia, Turkey-in-Europe, N Iran
J F M A **M J** J A S O N D

Fig 648
Cephalanthera kotschyana
Termessos, S Anatolia
Dist: N, S and E Anatolia
J F M A **M J** J A S O N D

Fig 649
Cephalanthera epipactoides
Nr. Eğridir, C Anatolia
Dist: Turkey-in-Europe, Outer Anatolia, Islands
J F M **A M J** J A S O N D

237

Orchidaceae: *Cephalanthera/Epipactis*

Cephalanthera kurdica
Nr. Artvin, NE Anatolia
Dist: NE, E and S Anatolia
J F M **A M** J J A S O N D

Cephalanthera rubra
Nr. Akseki, S Anatolia
Dist: Widespread except SE in Anatolia, N and NW Iran
J F M A M **J J** A S O N D

Epipactis palustris
Çam Pass, NE Anatolia
Dist: N Turkey, E Anatolia, NW Iran
J F M A M J **J** A S O N D

Epipactis veratrifolia
Çoruh Valley, NE Anatolia
Dist: E and S Anatolia, N and W Iran
J F M A M **J J** A S O N D

Orchidaceae: *Epipactis*

Epipactis helleborine
Nr. Artvin, NE Anatolia
Dist: Widespread in Anatolia, except SE
J F M A M **J J** A S O N D

Epipactis pontica
Nr. Rize, NE Anatolia
Dist: N Anatolia
J F M A M J **J A** S O N D

Epipactis pontica
Nr. Rize, NE Anatolia
Dist: N Anatolia
J F M A M J **J A** S O N D

Orchidaceae: *Neottia/Limodorum/Epipogium/Goodyera/Spiranthes/Plantanthera*

Neottia

Neottia nidus-avis (bird's-nest orchid) **(Fig. 657)** is a saprophytic orchid found in deciduous forests (beech) in Anatolia and N Iran.

Limodorum

Limodorum abortivum **(Figs. 659, 660)** is another saprophytic species which is most often found in pine forests, but it grows in a range of habitats including oak scrub and macchie. It is distributed widely in Anatolia but is found less commonly in N and W Iran.

Epipogium

Epipogium aphyllum **(Fig. 658)** is another of the saprophytic species and is the rarest of the three, only occurring in a few places in N Anatolia. It grows in dense beech and coniferous woodland where there is very little ground cover.

Goodyera

Goodyera repens **(Fig. 661)** is found in the eastern half of N Anatolia growing in mossy places in woodland.

Spiranthes

Spiranthes spiralis **(Fig. 662)** is widely distributed in Europe, and in this area it is found in Outer Anatolia, and rarely in N Iran. It flowers late in the year (typically September and October) in grassy places and in open forest areas.

Plantanthera

Both ***Platanthera chlorantha*** **(Fig. 663)** and *Platanthera bifolia* are widely distributed in Anatolia and they are also found in N and W Iran.

An interesting form of *P. chlorantha* is found in Turkey, ***P. chlorantha* ssp. *holmboei*** **(Fig. 664)**, and this grows in open woodland in the Hatay area of S Anatolia, and in one or two places in SW Anatolia and the Islands. It has an eastern Mediterranean distribution from Lesbos to Cyprus and Israel.

Orchidaceae: *Neottia/Epipogium/Limodorum*

Fig 657
Neottia nidus-avis
Çam Pass, NE Anatolia
Dist: NW Turkey, N and S Anatolia, N Iran
J F M A M **J J** A S O N D

Fig 658
Epipogium aphyllum
Çam Pass, NE Anatolia
Dist: N Anatolia (rare)
J F M A M J **J A** S O N D

Fig 659
Limodorum abortivum
Island of Lesbos
Dist: Widespread except Inner Anatolia, N and W Iran
J F **M A M J** J A S O N D

Fig 660
Limodorum abortivum
Nr. Maraş, S Anatolia
Dist: Widespread except Inner Anatolia, N and W Iran
J F **M A M J** J A S O N D

Orchidaceae: *Goodyera/Spiranthes/Platanthera*

Goodyera repens
Nr. Artvin, NE Anatolia
Dist: N Anatolia
J F M A M J **J A S O** N D

Spiranthes spiralis
Tahtali Dağ, S Anatolia
Dist: Outer Anatolia, N Iran (rare)
J F M A M J J A **S O N D**

Platanthera chlorantha
Nr. Mardin, S Anatolia
Dist: Widespread in Anatolia, Islands, W Iran
J F M A M **J J** A S O N D

Platanthera chlorantha ssp. holmboei
Cyprus
Dist: S and SW Anatolia, Islands
J F M A **M J** J A S O N D

Ophrys

This family of orchids probably gives the greatest problems in terms of identification of plants in the Mediterranean region. It is made complicated by the variability of some species and their ability to produce hybrid populations, but is not helped by the proliferation of new species which are described in each new publication. Many of these are very localised forms.

This account deals with the more established species in each of the main groups and concentrates on their distribution in our area, but does not provide detailed descriptions. Most species occur round the outer fringes of Anatolia, particularly along the Mediterranean coasts and on the Islands. About 60 species have been described from Turkey and 10 from Iran.

The shape, colour and marking of the lip of the flower, and the colour of the sepals are usually the most recognisable features of *Ophrys* species. These orchids are pollinated by insects such as wasps and hover-flies and the nature of the lip controls the particular insect that is attracted to the flower.

The Ophrys fusca group

This group has always been considered as very variable, and accepted species in this group, such as **Ophrys fusca (Fig. 665)** itself, **Ophrys omegaifera (Fig. 666)**, **Ophrys iricolor (Fig. 667)** and **Ophrys israelitica (Fig. 668)** have been recognised for some time. More recently many other variations have been described and three are illustrated here, **O. cinereophylla (Fig. 669)**, **O. blitopertha (Fig. 670)** and **O. attavira (Fig. 671)**. Most of these species are found in macchie close to the coast in SW Anatolia and the Islands.

The Ophrys lutea group

It is now recognised that *Ophrys lutea* itself does not occur in Turkey, the species present being **O. sicula (Fig. 672)** and **O. phryganae (Fig. 673)**. The former is more common and widely distributed and has small, yellow-edged flowers with a distinctive brown triangle at the base of the lip. *O. phryganae* has larger flowers, similar to those of *O. lutea*, with a broad, yellow-brown edging.

The Ophrys sphegodes group

As with the previous group *Ophrys sphegodes* is not now recognised from Turkey, with the group represented by species such as **O. caucasica (Fig. 674)**, **O. sintenisii (Fig. 675)**, **O. transhyrcana (Fig. 676)** and **O. mammosa (Fig. 677)**. Of these species *O. mammosa* is the most common, both in Turkey and elsewhere. *O. transhyrcana* is closely related and like *O. mammosa* it has distinct lobes at the sides of the lip, but the lip of the former has a more triangular shape. It is only found in S and SE Anatolia. *O. sintenisii* is restricted to N Anatolia in the Pontic Alps and along the Black Sea coast, where it grows in phrygana and other bushy places. *O. caucasica* is endemic to the Pontic Alps area of N Anatolia, particularly growing in grassy places amongst the hazel groves. Other species in this group include *O. pseudomammosa* and *O. hittiaca*.

The Ophrys scolopax group

Four species of this type are illustrated, **Ophrys bremifera (Fig. 678)**, **O. oestrifera (Fig. 679)**, **O. minutula (Fig. 680)** and **O. lapethica (Fig. 681)**. *Ophrys bremifera* is found quite widely in Outer Anatolia from the hazel groves of Trabzon in the NE to the coastal phrygana of the SW. *O. oestrifera* has very long lateral lobes to the lip (hornlike) which led to the old name *O. scolopax ssp. cornuta*. It is widely distributed in macchie and phrygana in Outer Anatolia and the Islands. *O. minutula* has very small flowers and is restricted to the Izmir area of W Anatolia and the Islands. *O. lapethica* is found in a few places in the Antalya and Hatay areas of S Anatolia, its main distribution being in Cyprus. It is another species with rather small flowers.

Ophrys phrygia is an endemic member of this group which is quite widely distributed in Inner, S and SE Anatolia. It is similar in appearance to *O. heldreichii* from Greece and Crete.

The Ophrys umbilicata group

Three species from this group are shown, **Ophrys umbilicata (Fig. 682)**, **Ophrys attica (Fig. 683)** and **Ophrys rhodia (Fig. 684)**. With all species in this group the central sepal is strongly curved over the flowers. *Ophrys umbilicata* is a relatively common but variable species from W and S Anatolia, and it is found in coastal phrygana. *O. attica* is much more restricted, only occurring in the Adana area of S Anatolia. *O. rhodia* has smaller flowers than the other species and is restricted to the island of Rhodes.

Other species in this group include *O. bucephala*, *O. khuzestanica* and *O. abchasica*.

Orchidaceae: *Ophrys*

The *Ophrys bornmuelleri* group

Ophrys bornmuelleri **(Fig. 685)** is an eastern Mediterranean species which is found in the Hatay area, and in a few places in E Anatolia, where it grows in open woodland and bushy places. ***O. ziyaretiana*** **(Fig. 686)** is very similar but it has much smaller flowers, and is again found in the Hatay area. ***O. levantina*** **(Fig. 687)** has a wider distribution, occurring in the İçel, Adana and Hatay areas, islands such as Rhodes, and a few places in SE Anatolia.

Another species, *O. carduchorum*, is restricted to SE Anatolia.

The *Ophrys reinholdii* group

Ophrys reinholdii **(Fig. 688)** is a distinctive species found in macchie, phrygana and oak scrub in W and SW Anatolia and the Islands. Closely related to this is ***O. straussii*** **(Fig. 689)** which has a lip with very strong, white markings. It has a wider distribution in E and S Anatolia and SW Iran. A variety of this, *O. straussii var. leucotaenia*, with white-haired side lobes to the lip, is recognised from the Antalya and İçel areas of S Anatolia.

Ophrys antiochiana **(Fig. 690)** is a related species which is only found locally in the Antakya region of S Anatolia.

The *Ophrys holoserica* group

Ophrys holoserica **(Fig. 691)** is a very widely distributed species extending from the U.K. to the eastern Mediterranean. In our area it grows in Turkey-in-Europe, W and S Anatolia and the Islands, and is found in macchie, phrygana and open woodland. A very large-flowered form which used to be called *O. holoserica ssp. maxima*, and is now ***O. episcopalis*** **(Fig. 692)** is found in the Muğla, İçel and Hatay areas of S Anatolia, and on islands such as Rhodes. Another closely related species, ***O. candica*** **(Fig. 693)**, is restricted to SW Anatolia and the Islands, where it grows in light woodland, macchie and phrygana.

Ophrys heterochila **(Fig. 694)** has rather smaller and less strongly-coloured flowers, and is quite widely found in SW and S Anatolia and the Islands.

Ophrys minoa **(Fig. 695)** is one of a number of more recently described forms, which grows in the Antalya area of S Anatolia. Other species include *O. calypsus* and *O. homeri*.

The *Ophrys ferrum-equinum* group

Ophrys ferrum-equinum **(Fig. 696)** has a distinct, horseshoe-shaped marking on the lip and is found in grassy and bushy places in W and S Anatolia and the Islands. A form of this with a narrower lip, ***O. ferrum-equinum ssp. labiosum*** **(Fig. 697)**, has a more local distribution in SW Anatolia and on some of the Islands.

Another species, ***Ophrys lucis*** **(Fig. 698)**, is found in S and SW Anatolia and islands such as Rhodes, where it is most often found growing in light woodland.

Other *Ophrys* species

Ophrys tenthredinifera (Figs. 645, 699)
This widespread Mediterranean species grows on limestone slopes, macchie and phrygana in W Anatolia and on the Islands.

Ophrys apifera (Fig. 700)
The familiar bee orchid grows in many places in this area, particularly in grassy meadows on hillsides along the Black Sea coast of N Anatolia, but it is also found in the SW and on the Islands.

Ophrys cilicica (Fig. 701)
This is a distinct, narrow-lipped *Ophrys* with a very localised distribution in S and SE Anatolia. It grows in damp places at the edge of fields or amongst limestone rocks.

Other very localised species include *O. schulzei*, which has a very small lip, and grows in the Amanus and Mesopotamian regions of S and SE Anatolia, and the endemic *O. isaura* from the İçel area.

Two endemic species from Iran are *O. kurdestanica* (NW) and *O. turcomanica* (N).

Ophrys speculum (Fig. 702)
The very attractive mirror orchid has a strong, blue patch in the centre of the lip, hence its name. It occurs throughout the Mediterranean region and is found here in Turkey-in-Europe, W and S Anatolia and the Islands.

Ophrys regis-ferdinandii (Fig. 703)
This is often considered as a subspecies of *Ophrys speculum* and has very narrow-lipped flowers with a small blue patch. It only occurs along the western Mediterranean coast in Turkey-in-Europe, W Anatolia and the Islands, where it grows in open macchie and woodland.

Ophrys bombyliflora (Fig. 704)
This is another very widespread species which is found in Turkey-in-Europe, SW Anatolia and the Islands. It grows in damp, sandy and grassy places and has small flowers with rather broad, yellow-green sepals.

Orchidaceae: *Ophrys*

Ophrys fusca
Island of Lesbos
Dist: SW Anatolia, Islands
J F **M A M** J J A S O N D

Ophrys omegaifera
Island of Rhodes
Dist: SW Anatolia, Islands
J F **M A** M J J A S O N D

Ophrys iricolor
Island of Chios
Dist: SW and S Anatolia
J F **M A M** J J A S O N D

Ophrys israelitica
Nr. Antakya, S Anatolia
Dist: S Anatolia
J F **M A M** J J A S O N D

Orchidaceae: *Ophrys*

Ophrys cinereophila
Island of Chios
Dist: SW Anatolia, Islands
J F **M A** M J J A S O N D

Ophrys blitopertha
Island of Chios
Dist: SW Anatolia, Islands
J F **M A** M J J A S O N D

Ophrys attavira
Island of Chios
Dist: SW Anatolia, Islands
J F **M A** M J J A S O N D

Ophrys sicula
Island of Rhodes
Dist: NW Turkey, W and S Anatolia, Islands
J F **M A** M J J A S O N D

Orchidaceae: *Ophrys*

Ophrys phryganae
Nr. Bodrum, SW Anatolia
Dist: SW Anatolia
J F M **A** M J J A S O N D

Ophrys caucasica
Nr. Trabzon, NE Anatolia
Dist: NE Anatolia
J F M A **M** J J A S O N D

Ophrys sintenisii
Cyprus
Dist: N Anatolia, N Iran
J F M A **M** J J A S O N D

Ophrys transhyrcana
Lake Van, SE Anatolia
Dist: S and SE Anatolia
J F M A **M** J J A S O N D

247

Orchidaceae: *Ophrys*

Fig 677

Ophrys mammosa
Nr. Akseki, S Anatolia
Dist: Turkey-in-Europe, W and S Anatolia
J F **M A M** J J A S O N D

Fig 678

Ophrys bremifera
Nr. Trabzon, NE Anatolia
Dist: Scattered in Outer Anatolia
J F M **A M** J J A S O N D

Fig 679

Ophrys oestrifera
Muğla, SW Anatolia
Dist: Outer Anatolia, Islands, N Iran
J F M **A M J** J A S O N D

Fig 680

Ophrys minutula
Island of Chios
Dist: W Anatolia, Islands
J F M **A M** J J A S O N D

Orchidaceae: *Ophrys*

Fig 681

Ophrys lapethica
N Cyprus
Dist: S Anatolia (rare)
J F M **A M** J J A S O N D

Fig 682

Ophrys umbilicata
Nr. Adana, S Anatolia
Dist: W and S Anatolia, W Iran
J F **M A M** J J A S O N D

Fig 683

Ophrys attica
Nr. Osmaniye, S Anatolia
Dist: S Anatolia (Maraş)
J F **M A** M J J A S O N D

Fig 684

Ophrys rhodia
Island of Rhodes
Dist: Rhodes
J F **M A** M J J A S O N D

Orchidaceae: *Ophrys*

Ophrys bornmuelleri
N Cyprus
Dist: S Anatolia (Hatay area), E Anatolia
J F **M A M** J J A S O N D

Ophrys ziyaretiana
Nr. Antakya, S Anatolia
Dist: S Anatolia (Hatay area)
J F **M A M** J J A S O N D

Ophrys levantina
Island of Rhodes
Dist: S and SE Anatolia, Islands
J F **M A M** J J A S O N D

Ophrys reinholdii
Island of Rhodes
Dist: SW Anatolia, Islands
J F **M A M** J J A S O N D

Orchidaceae: *Ophrys*

Fig 689

Fig 690

Ophrys straussii
Nr. Gaziantep, S Anatolia
Dist: **S and SE Anatolia, NW Iran**
J F M **A M** J J A S O N D

Ophrys antiochiana
Nr. Antakya, S Anatolia
Dist: **S Anatolia (Hatay area)**
J F M **A M** J J A S O N D

Fig 691

Fig 692

Ophrys holoserica
Muğla, SW Anatolia
Dist: **SW and S Anatolia**
J F M **A M** J J A S O N D

Ophrys episcopalis
Island of Rhodes
Dist: **SW and S Anatolia, Islands**
J F M **A M** J J A S O N D

251

Orchidaceae: *Ophrys*

Fig 693

Ophrys candica
Island of Rhodes
Dist: SW Anatolia, Islands
J F **M A** M J J A S O N D

Fig 694

Ophrys heterochila
Island of Chios
Dist: SW Anatolia, Islands
J F **M A** M J J A S O N D

Fig 695

Ophrys minoa
Nr. Antalya, S Anatolia
Dist: S Anatolia
J F **M A M** J J A S O N D

Fig 696

Ophrys ferrum-equinum
Island of Rhodes
Dist: SW and S Anatolia, Islands
J F **M A M** J J A S O N D

Orchidaceae: *Ophrys*

Ophrys ferrum-equinum ssp. *labiosum*
Island of Chios
Dist: SW Anatolia, Islands
J F **M A** M J J A S O N D

Ophrys lucis
Island of Rhodes
Dist: SW and S Anatolia, Islands
J F **M A** M J J A S O N D

Ophrys tenthredinifera
Island of Chios
Dist: W Turkey, SW Anatolia, Islands
J F **M A** M J J A S O N D

Ophrys apifera
Nr. Trabzon, NE Anatolia
Dist: Turkey-in-Europe, Outer Anatolia, Islands, N Iran
J F M A **M** J J A S O N D

253

Orchidaceae: *Ophrys*

Ophrys cilicica
Nr. Eğridir, S Anatolia
Dist: S and SE Anatolia
J F **M A M** J J A S O N D

Ophrys speculum
Island of Rhodes
Dist: Turkey-in-Europe, W and S Anatolia, Islands
J F **M A M** J J A S O N D

Ophrys regis-ferdinandii
Island of Rhodes
Dist: Turkey-in-Europe, W Anatolia, Islands
J F **M A M** J J A S O N D

Ophrys bombyliflora
Island of Rhodes
Dist: Turkey-in-Europe, W Anatolia, Islands
J F **M A M** J J A S O N D

Orchidaceae: *Serapias*

Serapias

The tongue orchids are well represented in the area with six species present in Turkey, but none in Iran. The flowers all have a long, pointed, brown lip that gives them their name.

Serapias bergonii (Fig. 705)
This is the species that was for many years called *Serapias vomeracea ssp. laxiflora* and it seems to be the eastern form of *Serapias vomeracea*. It occurs in Turkey-in-Europe, NW Turkey, SW and S Anatolia as far east as Hatay, and on the Islands.

Serapias politisii (Fig. 706)
This is a very small-flowered *Serapias* with long, narrow bracts and flowers with a lip that is bent back. It is only found in SW Anatolia and the Islands.

Serapias cordigera (Fig. 707)
This species has large flowers with a relatively wide, heart-shaped lip. It grows in the Istanbul region and in the extreme SW (Muğla) area, and is also found on the island of Lesbos. It favours grassy places, cultivated terraces and semi-shade on acid soils.

Serapias orientalis (Fig. 708)
This is another species with relatively large flowers, which is most common in regions such as Crete and S Greece. It occurs here in W and SW Anatolia and the Islands in grassland, cultivated terraces and olive groves, but always on alkaline soils.

Serapias levantina (Fig. 709)
This is a species with a strongly eastern distribution and it is found in two areas, in Hatay near the Syrian border, and around Diyarbakir in the SE. It grows on dry, stony hillsides and in poor grassland.

Serapias feldweggiana (Fig. 710)
This is an endemic species which occurs all along the Black Sea coast, particularly in the Trabzon and Ordu areas. It is the only species in this area and has brick red flowers.

Serapias bergonii
Island of Chios
Dist: NW Turkey, SW and S Anatolia, Islands
J F M **A M** J J A S O N D

Serapias politisii
Muğla, SW Anatolia
Dist: SW Anatolia, Islands
J F M **A M** J J A S O N D

Orchidaceae: *Serapias*

Fig 707

Fig 708

Serapias cordigera
Island of Lesbos
Dist: NW Turkey, SW Anatolia, Islands
J F **M A M** J J A S O N D

Serapias orientalis
Island of Rhodes
Dist: W and S Anatolia, Islands
J F **M A** M J J A S O N D

Fig 709

Fig 710

Serapias levantina
Nr. Antakya, S Anatolia
Dist: S and SE Anatolia
J F M **A M J** J A S O N D

Serapias feldweggiana
Nr. Rize, NE Anatolia
Dist: N and NE Anatolia
J F M A **M J** J A S O N D

Orchidaceae: *Aceras/Himantoglossum/Barlia/Neotinea/Traunsteinera/Steveniella/Comperia*

Aceras

The man orchid, ***Aceras anthropophorum* (Fig. 711)**, is found over a large geographical area from northern Europe to the Mediterranean, but in Turkey it is relatively rare, being found only in SW Anatolia and the Islands.

Himantoglossum

Three species of lizard orchid are present, *Himantoglossum caprinum, H. affine* and *H. montis-tauri*, and one, *H. affine*, extends into Iran. They all have flowers with a very long, twisted lip, which gives them their name.

Himantoglossum caprinum (Fig. 712)
This attractive species is found in N and NW Turkey in open woodland and scrub. The lip of the flower is dark purple in colour and has a greenish hood. It is a relatively large orchid and can be up to 1m tall.

The other two species are not illustrated, but *H. affine* is a less impressive plant with smaller, greenish-brown flowers. It is mainly found in Outer and Central Anatolia, particularly in the S and E, but also grows in Iran. The third species, *H. montis-tauri*, is very localised and has been found in the Termessos and Akseki areas of S Anatolia, and on the island of Lesbos. It has rather fewer, greenish-brown flowers, which are intermediate between *H. affine* and *H. caprinum*.

Barlia

The only species in the area, ***Barlia robertiana* (Fig. 713)**, is a common Mediterranean orchid and it is found in W and SW Anatolia and the Islands. It is a tall orchid (up to 80cm) with large basal leaves, flowering early in the spring. The large flowers are purplish or brownish-green, and the plant grows in macchie, phrygana and open woodland.

Neotinea

The representative of this genus, ***Neotinea maculata* (Fig. 714)**, has a head of very small white or pinkish flowers and a rosette of broad leaves, which are often brown spotted. It is generally found in the Mediterranean region of our area in NW Turkey, W and S Anatolia and the Islands. It is a plant of coniferous woodland and scrubby hillsides.

Traunsteinera

The only species in the area, ***Traunsteinera sphaerica* (Fig. 715)**, has a globular head of white flowers and is only found in NE Anatolia, where it grows in mountain pastures and meadows at about 2,000m.

Steveniella

The only species, ***Steveniella satyroides* (Fig. 716)**, has green-lipped flowers with a purplish hood, and they are quite small. The plant has a single leaf, and it is found in forest, oak scrub and hazel groves in N Anatolia and N Iran.

Comperia

This is another genus with a single species in the area, ***Comperia comperiana* (Figs. 717, 718)**, and this is probably the most unusual of all the orchids. The flowers have long, pendulous lobes on the lip, which makes them unmistakeable. The plant is up to 60cm tall and grows in mountain woodland and oak scrub in Outer and SE Anatolia and the Islands.

Orchidaceae: Aceras/Himantoglossum/Barlia/Neotinea

Aceras anthropophorum
Muğla, SW Anatolia
Dist: SW Anatolia, Islands
J F **M A** M J J A S O N D

Himantoglossum caprinum
Ulu Dağ, NW Turkey
Dist: N and NW Turkey
J F M A M J **J** A S O N D

Barlia robertiana
Island of Rhodes
Dist: W and S Anatolia, Islands
J **F M A** M J J A S O N D

Neotinea maculata
Island of Rhodes
Dist: NW Turkey, W and S Anatolia
J F **M A M** J J A S O N D

Orchidaceae: *Traunsteinera/Steveniella/Comperia*

Traunsteinera sphaerica
Pontic Alps, NE Anatolia
Dist: NE Anatolia
J F M A M **J J** A S O N D

Steveniella satyroides
Nr. Trabzon, NE Anatolia
Dist: N Anatolia, N and NW Iran
J F M **A M** J J A S O N D

Comperia comperiana
Lake Van, SE Anatolia
Dist: Outer and SE Anatolia, Islands
J F M A **M J J** A S O N D

Comperia comperiana
Nr Eğridir, S Anatolia
Dist: Outer and SE Anatolia, Islands
J F M A **M J J** A S O N D

Orchidaceae: *Orchis*

Orchis

Many of the *Orchis* species in this area are well-known from the wider Mediterranean region, but some, such as *O. caucasica, O. stevenii, O. adeinocheila, O. spitzelii* or *O. punctulata,* are endemic or much more restricted in their distribution. This genus contains some of the most spectacular orchids, some of which are quite large. Once again the size of the plant, the shape and colouring of the lip, and the overall flower colour are important characteristics..

Orchis italica (Fig. 719)
This is a common orchid in the Mediterranean region and its distribution in our area follows this, as it only occurs in SW and S Anatolia as far east as Hatay. It has pink flowers with a spotted lip in the shape of a man, and it grows in macchie and grassy places.

Orchis papilionacea (Fig. 720)
The so-called pink butterfly orchid is another that is widely distributed. Three forms in Turkey have been proposed, **v. papilionacea**, in Turkey-in-Europe and N Anatolia, **v. heroica** in SW Anatolia and the Islands, and **v. schirwanica** in S Anatolia and N Iran (*O. caspia*). The differences between them are small and they are largely defined by distribution.

Orchis lactea (Fig. 721)
The next two species are easily confused but in general *O. lactea* is a shorter plant (up to 15cm) which flowers earlier than *O. tridentata*. The purple-spotted lobes of the lip are squarer and the flower spike is more elongated. It only occurs in grassy places in W Turkey and on the Islands.

Orchis tridentata (Fig. 722)
This species has a much wider distribution than *O. lactea* occurring in NW Turkey, in most areas of Outer Anatolia and in W and NW Iran. It is 15-45cm tall and has a rather globular head of many, densely-packed flowers. These are given a rather sharp appearance by the pointed petals forming the hood. It grows in grassy places, macchie and scrub.

Orchis purpurea (Fig. 723)
The familiar lady orchid is most often found in N and W Anatolia, but it does not go further east than Ordu. It is a large plant (up to 80cm) with very large, broad leaves. The name is said to come from the shape of the lip which resembles a Victorian lady in crinoline. It grows in open places in woodland on calcareous soils.

Orchis caucasica (Fig. 724)
This is a very similar species which replaces *O. purpurea* in NE Anatolia, occurring most commonly around Trabzon and Artvin. It has flowers with a narrower lip and a more purple hood, and grows in hazel groves and light woodland.

Orchis adeinocheila (Figs. 725,726)
This is again related to *O. purpurea* but the flower colour is creamy-brown with a purple-spotted lip and a brown, purple-veined hood. It grows in light, deciduous woodland in N and NE Iran.

Orchis punctulata (Fig. 727)
This is another tall orchid (up to 70cm) and it has a strongly eastern distribution. In the Mediterranean region it extends as far west as E Greece and Cyprus, and in our area it grows in Outer Anatolia and N and NW Iran. The flowers are yellow with a flower shape very similar to that of *O. militaris* and it occurs in open scrub and forest.

Orchis stevenii (not illustrated)
This orchid is closely related to *O. militaris* which does not occur in our area. The flowers have a similar shape and colour to the military orchid, but the lip is much smaller and narrower. It is found in NE Anatolia, particularly in the Trabzon region, and in N and NW Iran, growing in mountain meadows.

Orchis simia (Fig. 728)
The familiar monkey orchid occurs widely in Outer Anatolia and N and NW Iran, though it is not common anywhere. It is a smaller plant than the previous species with pale pink, purple-spotted flowers and purple tips to the lobes of the lip. These turn up at the ends and give the flower its monkey-like appearance. It is found on grassy hillsides with calcareous soil.

Orchis spitzelii (Figs. 729–730)
This attractive orchid has a very disjunct distribution in Europe and North Africa, but it probably has more localities in Turkey than anywhere else, particularly in Outer Anatolia. It grows in open pine forests and has pink to purple flowers with a brown hood.

Orchis syriaca (Fig. 731)
This orchid is part of the *Orchis morio* group, and in the past it was considered to be a subspecies of *O. morio*. It is quite common in areas such as Cyprus, Syria and Lebanon and the Turkish distribution mirrors this, as it is only found in S and SW Anatolia. It has the green-veined hood of *O. morio* but the pink or mauve lip is unspotted. It grows in macchie, phrygana and light woodland.

O. morio does occur in Turkey but only in Turkey-in-Europe and N and NW Anatolia.

Orchis morio ssp. picta (Fig. 732)
This is the most common member of the *O. morio* complex in our area, and is found in Turkey-in-Europe, W and S Anatolia and N and NW Iran. It has a smaller flower than *O. morio* with a narrower lip that is strongly purple-spotted and with side lobes that are often turned down. It grows in similar habitats to *O. syriaca*.

Orchis pinetorum (Fig. 733)
This orchid is a tall form of *Orchis mascula* and was originally a subspecies of it. The bright purple flowers are in a rather lax spike and the leaves are unspotted. It grows in open places in forests and amongst oak scrub and is widespread throughout Anatolia, also occurring in N and NW Iran.

The normal *Orchis mascula* does grow in both Turkey and Iran, but it is more local and in Anatolia is mainly in the north.

The next set of closely-related species are in the *Orchis palustris* group and they are all tall plants favouring very wet meadows. They are purple-flowered and often grow in large numbers in suitable habitats.

Orchis palustris (Figs. 734, 735)
O. palustris is widespread in both Turkey and Iran, but is particularly common in central Anatolia. The flowers have a very broad, flat lip with a small central lobe and they are spotted in the centre. White-flowered forms **(Fig. 734)** occur quite commonly.

Orchis elegans (Fig. 736)
This is probably a particularly fine form of *O. palustris* which is found in the Antalya area of S Anatolia and near Lake Van in the SE. It is usually deep purple in colour and has a very broad lip with strong spotting down the centre.

Orchis pseudolaxiflora (Fig. 737)
This species has a rather more lax spike and the smaller flowers have a narrower lip which has a few central spots. It is mainly found in central and eastern Anatolia and usually occurs in large numbers.

Orchis laxiflora (Fig. 738)
This species has the broadest distribution in the Mediterranean region, but in Turkey it is mainly found in Outer Anatolia and the Islands. The purple flowers have no spots in the whitish centre to the lip, and the side lobes are often turned down, giving them a narrow appearance. It generally flowers a little earlier than the other species in the group.

A very local species, which occurs in the Hatay area, *O. dinsmorei*, is also in this group.

Orchis anatolica (Fig. 739)
This small orchid is 20-30cm tall and has up to ten, relatively large, pink flowers which have purple dots or lines down the centre of the lip. It grows in macchie, scrub and pinewoods, and is found quite commonly in W and S Anatolia and the Islands.

Orchis quadripunctata (Fig. 740)
This orchid is similar to *O. anatolica* but has up to 20 purple flowers on a stem, and these have 2 or 4 spots on the white centre of the lip. It grows in macchie, but is rare in Turkey, only occurring in a few places in W Anatolia and on the Islands.

Orchis provincialis (Fig. 741)
This is a yellow-flowered orchid with flowers that have small purple spots on the centre of the lip. It grows in open pine forests and scrub in scattered places in NW Anatolia and the Islands.

Orchis pallens (Fig. 742)
Orchis pallens is another yellow-flowered orchid, but it is a deeper yellow than *O. provincialis* and the flowers are unspotted. The habitat is also quite different, as it grows in mountain meadows and glades at above 1,000m.

Orchis coriophora (Fig. 743)
The bug orchid is very widely distributed in Anatolia except for the west, and also in W and NW Iran. It grows in wet meadows, often with other species such as *O. palustris* and *O. pseudolaxiflora*. It is about 30cm tall and has a spike of small, purple or greenish-red flowers.

Its subspecies, **ssp. fragrans (Fig. 744)**, is a Mediterranean species found in W Anatolia, S Anatolia as far east as Hatay, and the Islands. It grows in drier, sandy or open forest situations, and has slightly larger, red-purple flowers.

Orchis sancta (Fig. 745)
This is another Mediterranean species with a similar distribution and habitat preference to *O. coriophora* ssp. *fragrans*. These two species often grow together and hybridise quite readily, though *O. sancta* tends to start flowering a little later. It has a narrow spike of pink flowers.

Orchis collina (Fig. 746)
This species is one of the earliest to flower, and the 20-30cm stem has relatively few, purplish, greenish, or brownish flowers. It is found in grassy places in scattered areas of NW Turkey, SW Anatolia and the Islands, S Anatolia (Hatay region), and in N and NW Iran.

Orchidaceae: *Orchis*

Orchis italica
Island of Chios
Dist: SW and S Anatolia
J F **M A** M J J A S O N D

Orchis papilionacea v. heroica
Island of Lesbos
Dist: Outer Anatolia, Islands
J F **M A** M J J A S O N D

Orchis lactea
Island of Rhodes
Dist: W and NW Turkey, Islands
J **F M A** M J J A S O N D

Orchis tridentata
Nr. Trabzon, NE Anatolia
Dist: NW Turkey, Outer Anatolia, W and NW Iran
J F M **A M** J J A S O N D

Orchidaceae: *Orchis*

Orchis purpurea
Nr. Bagoren, C Anatolia
Dist: Turkey-in-Europe, C, N and W Anatolia
J F M **A M** J J A S O N D

Orchis caucasica
Nr. Artvin, NE Anatolia
Dist: NE Anatolia
J F M A **M J** J A S O N D

Orchis adeinocheila
Golestan, N Iran
Dist: N Iran
J F M **A** M J J A S O N D

Orchis adeinocheila
Golestan, N Iran
Dist: N Iran
J F M **A** M J J A S O N D

Orchidaceae: *Orchis*

Fig 727

Orchis punctulata
N Iran
Dist: Outer and Central E Anatolia, N Iran
J F M **A M** J J A S O N D

Fig 728

Orchis simia
Nr. Trabzon, NE Anatolia
Dist: Outer Anatolia, N and NW Iran
J F M **A M** J J A S O N D

Fig 729

Orchis spitzelii
Nr. Eğridir, S Anatolia
Dist: Outer Anatolia
J F M **A M** J J A S O N D

Fig 730

Orchis spitzelii
Nr. Eğridir, S Anatolia
Dist: Outer Anatolia
J F M **A M** J J A S O N D

Orchidaceae: *Orchis*

Orchis syriaca
Nr. Antalya, S Anatolia
Dist: S and SW Anatolia
J F **M A M** J J A S O N D

Orchis morio ssp. picta
Island of Chios
Dist: Turkey-in-Europe, W and S Anatolia, N and NW Iran
J F **M A M** J J A S O N D

Orchis pinetorum
Nr. Eğridir, S Anatolia
Dist: Outer Anatolia
J F M A **M J** J A S O N D

Orchis palustris (white form)
Lake Van, SE Anatolia
Dist: widespread in Turkey and Iran
J F M A M **J J** A S O N D

Orchidaceae: *Orchis*

Fig 735

Orchis palustris
Lake Van, SE Anatolia
Dist: widespread in Turkey and Iran
|J|F|M|A|M|**J**|**J**|A|S|O|N|D|

Fig 736

Orchis elegans
Nr. Lake Van, SE Anatolia
Dist: S and SE Anatolia
|J|F|M|A|**M**|**J**|J|A|S|O|N|D|

Fig 737

Orchis pseudolaxiflora
Nr. Artvin, NE Anatolia
Dist: C and E Anatolia
|J|F|M|A|**M**|**J**|**J**|A|S|O|N|D|

Fig 738

Orchis laxiflora
Island of Rhodes
Dist: Outer Anatolia, Islands
|J|F|M|**A**|**M**|J|J|A|S|O|N|D|

Orchidaceae: *Orchis*

Orchis anatolica
Island of Chios
Dist: W and S Anatolia, Islands, W Iran
J F **M A M** J J A S O N D

Orchis quadripunctata
Island of Lesbos
Dist: W Anatolia (rare), Islands
J F **M A M** J J A S O N D

Orchis provincialis
Island of Rhodes
Dist: NW Anatolia, Islands
J F **M A M** J J A S O N D

Orchis pallens
Zigana Pass, NE Anatolia
Dist: Outer Anatolia (rare in south)
J F **M A M** J J A S O N D

Orchidaceae: *Orchis*

Fig 743

Orchis coriophora
Lake Van, SE Anatolia
Dist: Widespread in Anatolia, W and NW Iran
|J|F|M|**A**|**M**|**J**|**J**|A|S|O|N|D|

Fig 744

Orchis coriophora* ssp. *fragrans
Island of Rhodes
Dist: W and S Anatolia, Islands
|J|F|M|**A**|**M**|**J**|J|A|S|O|N|D|

Fig 745

Orchis sancta
Island of Rhodes
Dist: SW and S Anatolia, Islands
|J|F|M|A|**M**|**J**|J|A|S|O|N|D|

Fig 746

Orchis collina
Island of Rhodes
Dist: NW Turkey, SW and S Anatolia, Islands, N and W Iran
|J|F|**M**|**A**|**M**|J|J|A|S|O|N|D|

Orchidaceae: Dactylorhiza

Dactylorhiza

The spotted and marsh orchid groups of the *Dactylorhiza* genus always cause problems of identification and this area is no exception. However many of the species in Turkey are endemic and occur in localised areas, so this helps in identification. The species generally fall into the groups recognised in the wider European area.

Dactylorhiza species are similar to many *Orchis* species, but one difference is that the bracts of *Dactylorhiza* are leaf-like and at least the lower ones often exceed the flowers, whereas those of *Orchis* are membranous and are closer to the flower colour. The species hybridise readily and this adds to identification problems. They often occur in large numbers, particularly in marshy situations.

Dactylorhiza iberica (Figs. 747,748)

This is one of the most distinctive species in the area, and it has small, rather widely spaced, pink or purple flowers. It is widespread in Anatolia in wet meadows and marshes, but is rare in SE Anatolia. It is also found in N and NW Iran.

The Dactylorhiza incarnata group

Dactylorhiza incarnata itself does occur in N and NW Anatolia but is rare and is not illustrated here. The yellow-flowered *D. ochroleuca* has been recorded in NW Iran.

Dactylorhiza osmanica (Figs. 749,750)

This is another species of marshy places, growing mainly in N, C and S Anatolia. It is stout and grows up to 60cm tall, with broad leaves and a dense, cylindrical spike of purple flowers which have a short, conical spur.

Dactylorhiza umbrosa (Figs. 751,752)

This closely-related species is most common in E and SE Anatolia and again grows in marshy meadows, often in very large numbers. It tends to be a smaller plant than *O. osmanica* with narrower leaves, and the bright purple flowers have a more pointed lip and a larger spur. It is also widespread in similar habitats in Iran.

The Dactylorhiza majalis group

Dactylorhiza majalis does not occur in the area and the only representative is *D.euxina*.

Dactylorhiza euxina (Figs. 753,754)

This is a shorter species (up to 30cm) which is found in marshes and wet meadows in the mountains of NE Anatolia. It has a hollow stem and narrow, black-spotted leaves. The short, dense spike has dark purple flowers with a fringed or irregularly-toothed lip.

The Dactylorhiza praetermissa group

The only representative of this group is the endemic *D. nieschalkiorum*, from damp meadows in mountains along the Black Sea coast in NW Anatolia. It is not illustrated.

The Dactylorhiza maculata group

This group has four representatives in Turkey, *D. saccifera*, *D. urvilleana*, *D. bithynica* and *D. ilgazica*, and one in Iran, *D. lancibracteata*. Only the first two species are illustrated. *D. ilgazica* and *D. lancibracteata* may well be the same, and are considered by some authors to be subspecies of *D. saccifera*. *D. bithynica* and *D. ilgazica* grow in damp areas and light woodland in NW and central N Anatolia.

Dactylorhiza saccifera (Figs. 755,756)

This orchid is up to 60cm tall with a solid stem and spotted leaves, and pink or white, purple-marked flowers. It is not common and grows in open forest and by streams in Outer Anatolia.

Dactylorhiza urvilleana (Figs. 757,758)

This species is found more frequently than the last, but only in N and NE Anatolia. It is another robust orchid that occurs in open woodland or in peaty alpine meadows. It again has purple-spotted leaves but has a hollow stem and darker pink flowers with a broader lip.

The Dactylorhiza romana group

There are two members of the group in the area and both occur with red or yellow flowers.

Dactylorhiza romana (Figs. 759,760)

This orchid has several, narrow leaves and a 20-30cm stem with a short spike of dull red or yellow flowers. The lip of the flower is unmarked and the spur is curved upwards. It grows in Turkey-in-Europe, Outer Anatolia and the Islands in macchie, oak scrub and open forest.

Dactylorhiza flavescens (Figs. 761,762)

This is a very similar species but it is only found in N and NE Anatolia and N and NW Iran. It has rather smaller flowers than *D. romana* and they are usually yellow, but purplish forms do also occur. The narrower spur of the flowers is more or less straight. It grows in open coniferous forest, oak scrub and alpine meadows.

Orchidaceae: *Dactylorhiza*

Dactylorhiza iberica
Çoruh Valley, NE Anatolia
Dist: Anatolia except SE, N and NW Iran
J F M A **M J J** A S O N D

Dactylorhiza iberica
Çam Pass, NE Anatolia
Dist: Anatolia except SE, N and NW Iran
J F M A **M J J** A S O N D

Dactylorhiza osmanica
Çam Pass, NE Anatolia
Dist: N, C and S Anatolia
J F M A M **J J** A S O N D

Dactylorhiza osmanica
Çam Pass, NE Anatolia
Dist: N, C and S Anatolia
J F M A M **J J** A S O N D

Orchidaceae: *Dactylorhiza*

Dactylorhiza umbrosa
Nr. Ardahan, NE Anatolia
Dist: E and SE Anatolia, widespread in Iran
J F M A M J J A S O N D

Dactylorhiza umbrosa
Nr. Lake Van, SE Anatolia
Dist: E and SE Anatolia, widespread in Iran
J F M A M J J A S O N D

Dactylorhiza euxina
Uzungöl, NE Anatolia
Dist: NE Anatolia
J F M A M J J A S O N D

Dactylorhiza euxina
Anzer Valley, NE Anatolia
Dist: NE Anatolia
J F M A M J J A S O N D

Orchidaceae: *Dactylorhiza*

Dactylorhiza saccifera
Nr. Rize, NE Anatolia
Dist: Scattered, mainly in N and NE Anatolia
J F M A M **J J** A S O N D

Dactylorhiza saccifera
Nr. Artvin, NE Anatolia
Dist: Scattered, mainly in N and NE Anatolia
J F M A M **J J** A S O N D

Dactylorhiza urvilleana
Zigana Pass, NE Anatolia
Dist: N and NE Anatolia
J F M A M **J J** A S O N D

Dactylorhiza urvilleana
Ovit Dağ, NE Anatolia
Dist: N and NE Anatolia
J F M A M **J J** A S O N D

Orchidaceae: *Dactylorhiza*

Dactylorhiza romana
Nr. Eğridir, S Anatolia
Dist: Turkey-in-Europe, Outer Anatolia, Islands
J F **A M** J J A S O N D

Dactylorhiza romana
Island of Lesbos
Dist: Turkey-in-Europe, Outer Anatolia, Islands
J F **A M** J J A S O N D

Dactylorhiza flavescens
Nr. Erzurum, E Anatolia
Dist: N and E Anatolia, N and NW Iran
J F **A M** J J A S O N D

Dactylorhiza flavescens
Golestan, N Iran
Dist: N and E Anatolia, N and NW Iran
J F **A M** J J A S O N D

Index

A

Aceras 257
   Aceras anthropophorum 257

Alliaceae 61

Allium 61
   Allium akaka 63
   Allium albidum ssp. *caucasicum* 61
   Allium albipilosum, see *Allium cristophii*
   Allium ampeloprasum 63
   Allium balansae 62
   Allium bodeanum 63
   Allium callidictyon 62
   Allium callimischon ssp. *haemostictum* 62
   Allium cardiostemon 63
   Allium carinatum ssp. *pulchellum* .. 62
   Allium cepa 62
   Allium cristophii 63
   Allium derderianum 63
   Allium fimbriatum, see *Allium callidictyon*
   Allium flavum 62
   Allium guttatum 63
   Allium hirtifolium 63
   Allium hymenorrhizum 61
   Allium junceum 63
   Allium kharputense 63
   Allium kurtzianum 62
   Allium myrianthum 63
   Allium neapolitanum 62
   Allium nigrum 63
   Allium noëanum 63
   Allium oreophilum 62
   Allium orientale 63
   Allium ostrowskianum, see *Allium oreophilum*
   Allium paradoxum 62
   Allium roseum 62
   Allium rubellum 62
   Allium schoenoprasum 61
   Allium shelkovnikovii 63
   Allium stamineum 62
   Allium subhirsutum 62
   Allium trifoliatum 62
   Allium triquetrum 62

Alrawia 111
   Alrawia bellii 111
   Alrawia nutans 111

Amaryllidaceae 173

Anemone 18
   Anemone biflora 18
   Anemone blanda 18
   Anemone caucasica 18
   Anemone coronaria 18
   Anemone pavonina 18
   Anemone petiolulosa 18
   Anemone tschernjaewi 18

Anthericum 60
   Anthericum liliago 60
   Anthericum ramosum 60

Araceae 43

Arisarum 52
   Arisarum vulgare 52

Arum 44
   Arum conophalloides, see *Arum detruncatum* v. *detruncatum*
   Arum creticum 44
   Arum detruncatum 44
      v. *caudatum* 44
      v. *detruncatum* 44
      v. *virescens* 44
   Arum dioscoridis 44
      v. *dioscoridis* 44
      v. *liepoldtii* 44
      v. *luschanii* 44
      v. *spectabile* 44
      v. *syriaca* 44
   Arum elongatum, see *Arum detruncatum* v. *virescens*
   Arum italicum 44
   Arum maculatum 44
   Arum nickelii 44
   Arum orientale 44

Asphodelaceae 53

Asphodeline 58
   Asphodeline baytopae 58
   Asphodeline brevicaulis 58
   Asphodeline damascena 58
      ssp. *ovoidea* 58
   Asphodeline liburnica 58
   Asphodeline lutea 58
   Asphodeline taurica 58

Asphodelus 53
   Asphodelus aestivus 53
   Asphodelus fistulosus 53
   Asphodelus ramosus 53
   Asphodelus tenuifolius 53

B

Barlia 257
   Barlia robertiana 257

Bellevalia 106
   Bellevalia dubia 106
   Bellevalia fominii 106
   Bellevalia forniculata 106
   Bellevalia gracilis 106
   Bellevalia kurdistanica 106
   Bellevalia longipes 106
   Bellevalia longistyla 106
   Bellevalia paradoxa 106
   Bellevalia pycnantha 106
   Bellevalia rixii 106
   Bellevalia tauri 106
   Bellevalia trifoliata 106
   Bellevalia tristis 106

Biarum 48
   Biarum bovei 48
   Biarum davisii 48
      ssp. *davisii* 48
      ssp. *marmarisensis* 48
   Biarum ditschianum 48
   Biarum eximium 48
   Biarum pyrami 48
   Biarum tenuifolium 48

Bongardia 25
   Bongardia chrysogonum 25

C

Cephalanthera 236
   Cephalanthera caucasica 236
   Cephalanthera damasonium 236
   Cephalanthera epipactoides 236
   Cephalanthera kotschyana 236
   Cephalanthera kurdica 236
   Cephalanthera longifolia 236
   Cephalanthera rubra 236

Chionodoxa 81
   Chionodoxa forbesii 81
   Chionodoxa luciliae 81
   Chionodoxa sardensis 81
   Chionodoxa siehei 81

Index

Chionodoxa tmoli 81
Colchicaceae 159
Colchicum 163
   Colchicum balansae 164
   Colchicum baytopiorum 164
   Colchicum bivonae 163
   Colchicum boissieri 164
   Colchicum bornmuelleri 163
   Colchicum burttii 163
   Colchicum chalcedonicum 163
   Colchicum cilicicum 163
   Colchicum decaisnei 164
   Colchicum dolichantherum 164
   Colchicum falcifolium,
      see *Colchicum serpentinum*
   Colchicum kotschyi 164
   Colchicum lingulatum 164
   Colchicum macrophyllum 163
   Colchicum micranthum 164
   Colchicum minutum 163
   Colchicum persicum 163
   Colchicum pusillum 164
   Colchicum sanguicolle 164
   Colchicum serpentinum 163
   Colchicum speciosum 163
   Colchicum stevenii 164
   Colchicum szovitsii 163
   Colchicum triphyllum 163
   Colchicum troodii, see *Colchicum
      decaisnei*
   Colchicum turcicum 163
   Colchicum umbrosum 164
   Colchicum variegatum 163
Comperia 257
   Comperia comperiana 257
Corydalis 27
   Corydalis alpestris 27
   Corydalis angustifolia 28
   Corydalis caucasica 28
   Corydalis chionophylla 27
      ssp. *firouzii* 27
   Corydalis conorhiza 27
   Corydalis erdelii 28
   Corydalis haussknechtii 28
   Corydalis henrikii 28
   Corydalis integra 28
   Corydalis lydica 28
   Corydalis marschalliana 28
   Corydalis nariniana 28
   Corydalis oppositifolia 27
   Corydalis paschei 28
   Corydalis solida 28
   Corydalis tauricola 28
   Corydalis triternata 28
   Corydalis verticillaris 28
   Corydalis wendelboi 28

Crocus 208
   Crocus abantensis 211
   Crocus adanensis 211
   Crocus aerius 211
   Crocus almehensis 210
   Crocus ancyrensis 210
   Crocus antalyensis 210
   Crocus asumaniae 208
   Crocus baytopiorum 211
   Crocus biflorus 210
      ssp. *adamii* 211
      ssp. *artvinensis* 210
      ssp. *biflorus* 210
      ssp. *crewei* 210
      ssp. *isauricus* 211
      ssp. *nubigena* 210
      ssp. *pseudonubigena* 211
      ssp. *pulchricolor* 210
      ssp. *punctatus* 210
      ssp. *tauri* 210
   Crocus cancellatus 208
      ssp. *cancellatus* 208
      ssp. *lycius* 208
      ssp. *mazziaricus* 208
   Crocus candidus 210
   Crocus cartwrightianus 208
   Crocus caspius 209
   Crocus chrysanthus 209
   Crocus danfordiae 209
   Crocus flavus 209
   Crocus fleischeri 210
   Crocus gargaricus 210
   Crocus gilanicus 208
   Crocus graveolens 209
   Crocus karduchorum 208
   Crocus kerndorffiorum 211
   Crocus kotschyanus 208
      ssp. *cappadocicus* 208
      ssp. *hakkariensis* 208
      ssp. *kotschyanus* 208
      ssp. *suworowianus* 208
   Crocus leichtlinii 211
   Crocus mathewii 208
   Crocus michelsonii 211
   Crocus nerimaniae 209
   Crocus olivieri 209
      ssp. *balansae* 209
      ssp. *istanbulensis* 209
      ssp. *olivieri* 209
   Crocus pallasii 208
      ssp. *dispathaceus* 208
      ssp. *haussknechtii* 208
      ssp. *pallasii* 208
   Crocus paschei, see *Crocus adanensis*
   Crocus pestalozzae 210
   Crocus pulchellus 209

   Crocus reticulatus 210
      ssp. *hittiticus* 210
      ssp. *reticulatus* 210
   Crocus sativus 208
   Crocus scharojanii ssp. *lazicus* 208
   Crocus sieheanus 210
   Crocus speciosus 209
      ssp. *ilgazensis* 209
      ssp. *speciosus* 209
   Crocus tournefortii 209
   Crocus vallicola 208
   Crocus vitellinus 209
   Crocus wattiorum 209
      ssp. *damascenus* 208
      ssp. *gargaricus* 210
      ssp. *herbertii* 210
      ssp. *pamphylicus* 208
      ssp. *xantholaimos* 209
Cyclamen 35
   Cyclamen alpinum 36
   Cyclamen cilicium 36
   Cyclamen coum 36
      ssp. *caucasicum* 36
   Cyclamen elegans 36
   Cyclamen graecum 35
      ssp. *anatolicum* 36
      ssp. *graecum* 36
   Cyclamen hederifolium 35
   Cyclamen intaminatum 36
   Cyclamen mirabile 36
   Cyclamen parviflorum 36
   Cyclamen persicum 36
   Cyclamen pseudibericum 36
   Cyclamen repandum ssp. *rhodense* 36
   Cyclamen trochopteranthum,
      see *Cyclamen alpinum*

D

Dactylorhiza 269
   Dactylorhiza bithynica 269
   Dactylorhiza euxina 269
   Dactylorhiza flavescens 269
   Dactylorhiza iberica 269
   Dactylorhiza ilgazica 269
   Dactylorhiza lancibracteata 269
   Dactylorhiza nieschalkiorum 269
   Dactylorhiza osmanica 269
   Dactylorhiza romana 269
   Dactylorhiza saccifera 269
   Dactylorhiza umbrosa 269
   Dactylorhiza urvilleana 269
Dipcadi 74
   Dipcadi serotinus 74
   Dipcadi susianum 74
   Dipcadi unicolor 74

Index

Dracunculus 52
    Dracunculus vulgaris 52

E

Eminium 51
    Eminium intortum 51
    Eminium koenenianum 51
    Eminium rauwolffii 51
    Eminium spiculatum 51
Epipactis 236
    Epipactis helleborine 236
    Epipactis palustris 236
    Epipactis pontica 236
    Epipactis veratrifolia 236
Epipogium 240
    Epipogium aphyllum 240
Eranthis 18
    Eranthis hyemalis 18
    Eranthis longistipitata 18
Eremurus 55
    Eremurus cappadocicus 55
    Eremurus inderiensis 55
    Eremurus kopetdaghensis 55
    Eremurus luteus 55
    Eremurus olgae 55
    Eremurus persicus 55
    Eremurus spectabilis 55
    Eremurus stenophyllus 55
Erythronium 150
    Erythronium caucasicum 150
    Erythronium dens-canis 150

F

Fritillaria 119
    Fritillaria acmopetala 119
    Fritillaria alburyana 120
    Fritillaria alfredae 120
    Fritillaria amana 119
    Fritillaria ariana 119
    Fritillaria armena 121
    Fritillaria assyriaca 121
        ssp. *melananthera* 121
    Fritillaria aurea 119
    Fritillaria bithynica 120
    Fritillaria carica 120
    Fritillaria caucasica 121
    Fritillaria chlororhabdota 121
    Fritillaria crassifolia 119
        ssp. *crassifolia* 119
        ssp. *hakkarensis* 120
        ssp. *kurdica* 119
    Fritillaria elwesii 121
    Fritillaria fleischeriana 120
    Fritillaria forbesii 120
    Fritillaria gibbosa 119
    Fritillaria imperialis 119
    Fritillaria kittaniae 121
    Fritillaria kotschyana 120
    Fritillaria latakiensis 121
    Fritillaria latifolia 119
    Fritillaria michailovskyi 119
    Fritillaria minima 121
    Fritillaria minuta 120
    Fritillaria olivieri 120
    Fritillaria pelinea 120
    Fritillaria persica 119
    Fritillaria pinardii 121
    Fritillaria pontica 119
    Fritillaria raddeana 119
    Fritillaria reuteri 119
    Fritillaria rhodia 120
    Fritillaria sibthorpiana 120
    Fritillaria sororum 120
    Fritillaria straussii 119
    Fritillaria stribrnyi 120
    Fritillaria uva-vulpis 121
    Fritillaria viridiflora 120
    Fritillaria whittallii 119
    Fritillaria zagrica 121
Fumariaceae 27

G

Gagea 151
    Gagea alexeenkoana 152
    Gagea bithynica 152
    Gagea bohemica 151
    Gagea bulbifera 151
    Gagea chomutowae 152
    Gagea confusa 152
    Gagea dschungarica 152
    Gagea fibrosa 151
    Gagea fistulosa 151
    Gagea gageoides 151
    Gagea glacialis 151
    Gagea graeca 151
    Gagea granatellii 151
    Gagea lutea 151
    Gagea luteoides 151
    Gagea olgae 152
    Gagea ova 152
    Gagea peduncularis 152
    Gagea stipitata 152
    Gagea taurica 151
    Gagea tenuifolia 152
    Gagea uliginosa 152
    Gagea vegeta 152
    Gagea villosa 152
Galanthus 177
    Galanthus alpinus 177
    Galanthus cilicicus 177
    Galanthus elwesii 177
    Galanthus fosteri 177
    Galanthus gracilis 177
    Galanthus koenenianus 177
    Galanthus nivalis 177
    Galanthus peshmenii 177
    Galanthus plicatus ssp.
        byzantinus 177
    Galanthus rizehensis 177
    Galanthus transcaucasicus 177
    Galanthus woronowii 177
Gladiolus 230
    Gladiolus anatolicus 230
    Gladiolus antakiensis 230
    Gladiolus atroviolaceus 230
    Gladiolus halophyllus 230
    Gladiolus humilis 230
    Gladiolus illyricus 230
    Gladiolus italicus 230
    Gladiolus kotschyanus 230
    Gladiolus micranthus 230
    Gladiolus persicus 230
    Gladiolus triphyllus 230
Goodyera 240
    Goodyera repens 240
Gynandriris 207
    Gynandriris sisyrinchium 207

H

Hermodactylus 207
    Hermodactylus tuberosus 207
Himantoglossum 257
    Himantoglossum affine 257
    Himantoglossum caprinum 257
    Himantoglossum montis-tauri 257
Hyacinthaceae 73
Hyacinthella 111
    Hyacinthella acutiloba 111
    Hyacinthella glabrescens 111
    Hyacinthella heldreichii 111
    Hyacinthella hispida 111
    Hyacinthella nervosa 111
    Hyacinthella persica 111
Hyacinthus 104
    Hyacinthus litwinowii 104
    Hyacinthus orientalis 104
    Hyacinthus transcaspicus 104

I

Iridaceae 185
Iris 186
    Iris acutiloba ssp. *lineolata* 188
    Iris albicans 187
    Iris aphylla 187
    Iris attica 187
    Iris aucheri 188
    Iris barnumae 187
        f. *barnumae* 187

Index

f. protonyma 187
f. urmiensis 187
Iris caucasica 188
Iris danfordiae 188
Iris drepanophylla 189
Iris fosteriana 189
Iris galatica 189
Iris gatesii 187
Iris germanica 186
Iris histrio 188
Iris histrioides 188
Iris hymenospatha 189
Iris iberica 187
ssp. elegantissima 187
ssp. lycotis 187
Iris imbricata 187
Iris kerneriana 186
Iris kirkwoodii 187
Iris kopetdagensis 189
Iris lazica 186
Iris masia 186
Iris meda 188
Iris meda hybrids 188
Iris mesopotamica 186
Iris orientalis 186
Iris pamphylica 188
Iris paradoxa 187
Iris persica 189
Iris pseudacorus 186
Iris pseudocaucasica 189
Iris purpureobractea 187
Iris reticulata 188
v. bakeriana 188
v. hyrcana 188
v. reticulata 188
Iris sari 188
Iris schachtii 187
Iris sibirica 186
Iris sintenisii 186
Iris songarica 186
Iris spuria ssp. musulmanica 186
Iris stenophylla 189
Iris suaveolens 187
Iris taochia 187
Iris unguicularis ssp. carica 186
ssp. caucasica 188
ssp. demawendica 187
ssp. turcica 188
Ixiolirion 181
Ixiolirion tataricum 181

L

Leontice 25
Leontice armenaica 25
Leontice leontopetalum 25
Leontice minor, see Leontice armenaica

Leucojum 176
Leucojum aestivum 176
Liliaceae 113
Lilium 114
Lilium akkusianum 114
Lilium candidum 114
Lilium carniolicum ssp. ponticum .114
Lilium ciliatum 114
Lilium kesselringianum 114
Lilium ledebourii 114
Lilium martagon 114
Lilium monadelphum 114
Lilium ponticum, see Lilium carniolicum ssp. ponticum
Limodorum 240
Limodorum abortivum 240

M

Merendera 160
Merendera attica 160
Merendera kurdica 160
Merendera raddeana 160
Merendera robusta 160
Merendera sobolifera 160
Merendera trigyna 160
Merendera wendelboi 160
Muscari 94
Muscari anatolicum 95
Muscari armeniacum 94
Muscari aucheri 94
Muscari azureum 95
Muscari bourgaei 95
Muscari caucasicum 94
Muscari chalusicum, see Muscari pseudomuscari
Muscari coeleste 95
Muscari commutatum 95
Muscari comosum 94
Muscari discolor 95
Muscari inconstrictum 95
Muscari latifolium 95
Muscari macbeathianum 95
Muscari macrocarpum 94
Muscari muscarimi 94
Muscari neglectum 95
Muscari parviflorum 95
Muscari pseudomuscari 95
Muscari sandrasicum 95
Muscari tenuiflorum 94
Muscari weissii 94

N

Narcissus 181
Narcissus serotinus 181
Narcissus tazetta 181
Nectaroscordum 72
Nectaroscordum koelzii 72

Nectaroscordum siculum ssp. bulgaricum 72
Nectaroscordum tripedale 72
Neotinea 257
Neotinea maculata 257
Neottia 240
Neottia nidus-avis 240

O

Ophrys 243
Ophrys antiochiana 244
Ophrys apifera 244
Ophrys attavira 243
Ophrys attica 243
Ophrys blitopertha 243
Ophrys bombyliflora 244
Ophrys bornmuelleri 244
Ophrys bremifera 243
Ophrys candica 244
Ophrys caucasica 243
Ophrys cilicica 244
Ophrys cinereophylla 243
Ophrys cornuta, see Ophrys oestrifera
Ophrys episcopalis 244
Ophrys ferrum-equinum 244
Ophrys ferrum-equinum ssp. labiosum 244
Ophrys heterochila 244
Ophrys holoserica ssp. maxima, see Ophrys episcopalis
Ophrys iricolor 243
Ophrys israelitica 243
Ophrys lapethica 243
Ophrys levantina 244
Ophrys lucis 244
Ophrys mammosa 243
Ophrys minoa 244
Ophrys minutula 243
Ophrys oestrifera 243
Ophrys omegaifera 243
Ophrys phryganae 243
Ophrys regis-ferdinandii 244
Ophrys reinholdii 244
Ophrys rhodia 243
Ophrys sicula 243
Ophrys sintenisii 243
Ophrys spcculum 244
Ophrys straussii 244
Ophrys tenthredinifera 244
Ophrys transhyrcana 243
Ophrys umbilicata 243
Ophrys ziyaretiana 244
Orchidaceae 235
Orchis 260
Orchis adeinocheila 260
Orchis anatolica 261
Orchis caspia 260

Index

Orchis caucasica 260
Orchis collina 261
Orchis coriophora 261
    ssp. *fragrans* 261
Orchis dinsmorei 261
Orchis elegans 261
Orchis italica 260
Orchis lactea 260
Orchis laxiflora 261
Orchis morio ssp. *picta* 261
Orchis pallens 261
Orchis palustris 261
Orchis papilionacea 260
    v. *heroica* 260
    v. *papilionacea* 260
    v. *schirwanica* 260
Orchis pinetorum 261
Orchis provincialis 261
Orchis pseudolaxiflora 261
Orchis punctulata 260
Orchis purpurea 260
Orchis quadripunctata 261
Orchis sancta 261
Orchis simia 260
Orchis spitzelii 260
Orchis stevenii 260
Orchis syriaca 260
Orchis tridentata 260

Ornithogalum 85
Ornithogalum alpigenum 86
Ornithogalum arabicum 86
Ornithogalum arcuatum 85
Ornithogalum armeniacum 85
Ornithogalum bungei 85
Ornithogalum comosum 85
Ornithogalum fimbriatum 85
Ornithogalum lanceolatum 86
Ornithogalum montanum 86
Ornithogalum narbonense 85
Ornithogalum nutans 86
Ornithogalum oligophyllum 86
Ornithogalum orthophyllum 86
Ornithogalum persicum 86
Ornithogalum platyphyllum 86
Ornithogalum pyrenaicum 85
Ornithogalum shelkovnikovii 85
Ornithogalum sigmoideum 86
Ornithogalum sintenisii 86
Ornithogalum sphaerocarpum 85
Ornithogalum ulophyllum 85
Ornithogalum umbellatum 86
Ornithogalum wiedemanniae 86

P

Pancratium 181
Pancratium maritimum 181

Plantanthera 240
    Platanthera chlorantha 240
        ssp. *holmboei* 240
Primulaceae 35
Puschkinia 83
    Puschkinia scilloides 83
    Puschkinia sp. 83

R

Ranunculus 18
    Ranunculus asiaticus 18
    Ranunculus cadmicus 18
    Ranunculus ficaria ssp. *calthifolia* .. 18
    Ranunculus kochii 18
    Ranunculus myosuroides 18
    Ranunculus unguis-cati 18
Romulea 228
    Romulea bulbocodium 228
        v. *bulbocodium* 228
        v. *crocea* 228
        v. *leichtliniana* 228
    Romulea columnae 228
    Romulea linaresii ssp. *graca* ...228
    Romulea ramiflora 228
    Romulea tempskyana 228

S

Scilla 75
    Scilla autumnalis 75
    Scilla bifolia 75
    Scilla bisotunensis 76
    Scilla bithynica 75
    Scilla cilicica 75
    Scilla gorganica 76
    Scilla greilhuberi 75
    Scilla hohenackeri 75
    Scilla hyacinthoides 75
    Scilla ingridae 76
    Scilla khorassanica 76
    Scilla leepii 76
    Scilla melaina 75
    Scilla mesopotamica 76
    Scilla mischtschenkoana 75
    Scilla monanthos 75
    Scilla persica 75
    Scilla rosenii 75
    Scilla siberica ssp. *armena* 75
    Scilla sp. 75
    Scilla tubergeniana, see *Scilla mischtschenkoana*
    Scilla winogradowii 75
Serapias 255
    Serapias bergonii 255
    Serapias cordigera 255
    Serapias feldweggiana 255
    Serapias levantina 255
    Serapias orientalis 255

    Serapias politisii 255
Spiranthes 240
    Spiranthes spiralis 240
Sternbergia 174
    Sternbergia candida 174
    Sternbergia clusiana 174
    Sternbergia colchiciflora 174
    Sternbergia fischeriana 174
    Sternbergia lutea 174
    Sternbergia sicula 174
Steveniella 257
    Steveniella satyroides 257

T

Traunsteinera 257
    Traunsteinera sphaerica 257
Tulipa 138
    Tulipa agenensis 138
    Tulipa armena 139
    Tulipa biebersteiniana 138
    Tulipa biflora 138
    Tulipa clusiana 138
    Tulipa hoogiana 139
    Tulipa humilis 138
    Tulipa julia 139
    Tulipa linifolia 139
    Tulipa micheliana 139
    Tulipa montana 138, 139
        v. *chrysantha* 138
    Tulipa mucronata 138
    Tulipa orphanidea 138
    Tulipa polychroma 138
    Tulipa praecox 138
    Tulipa saxatilis 138
    Tulipa schrenkii 139
    Tulipa sintenisii 139
    Tulipa sp. 139
    Tulipa sprengeri 139
    Tulipa stapfii, see *Tulipa systola*
    Tulipa sylvestris 138
    Tulipa systola 139
    Tulipa ulophylla 139
    Tulipa undulatifolia 139
    Tulipa urumiensis 138
    Tulipa violacea var. *pallida* .. 138
    Tulipa whittallii 138
    Tulipa wilsoniana 139

U

Ungernia 181
    Ungernia flava 181
    Ungernia severzovii 181
    Ungernia trisphaera 181
Urginea 74
    Urginea maritima 74

Bibliography

Flora of Turkey and the East Aegean Islands, Vols. 1-11, P. H. Davis (ed.), Edinburgh University Press (1984-2001).

Flora Iranica, Flora des Iranischen Hochlands und der Umrahmenden Gebirge, K. H. Rechinger (ed.), Academic Press, Graz, Austria.

- Vol. 1 Araceae
- Vol. 67 Amaryllidaceae
- Vol. 76 Alliaceae
- Vol. 112 Iridaceae
- Vol. 126 Orchidaceae
- Vol. 151 Liliaceae Parts I, II and III

Bulbous Plants of Turkey, B. Mathew and T. Baytop, Batsford and the Alpine Garden Society, 1984.

Bulbs, R. Phillips and M. Rix, Pan Books, 1989.

Mediterranean Wild Flowers, M. Blamey and C. Grey-Wilson, Harper Collins 1993.

Tulips and Irises of Iran, P. Wendelbo, Botanical Institute of Iran, 1977.

Corydalis, M. Liden and H. Zetterlund, AGS Publications Ltd., 1997.

The Crocus, B. Mathew, Batsford, 1982.

Crocus Update, B. Mathew, The Plantsman, March and June 2002, RHS Publications Ltd.

Cyclamen, a gardener's guide, C. Grey-Wilson, AGS Publications Ltd., 2006

Hardy Hyacinthaceae Parts 1,2 and 3, B. Mathew, The Plantsman, March, June and September 2005, RHS Publications Ltd.

A New Species of Lily from Turkey (describes and illustrates all the Lily species from Turkey), R. Gämperle, AGS Bulletin, Vol. 66, No. 3, Sept. 1998.

Die Orchideen der Türkei, C. A. J. Kreutz, Landgraaf, Holland, 1998.

Snowdrops, M. Bishop, A. Davis and J. Grimshaw, Griffin Press, 2001.

Tulips, R. Wilford, Timber Press, 2006.

Photographic Credits

The majority of the photographs in this book have been taken by the author, but many others have willingly contributed and are gratefully acknowledged. The photographic sources are listed below. Entries marked with an asterisk come from the Alpine Garden Society Slide Library.

Noel Allen*
233, 316, 375

Bill Baker*
563

Kath Baker*
465

H. Baumann*
265, 350, 564

Turhan Baytop
612

Kim Blaxland*
74, 330, 482

Ann Borrill*
114, 257, 504

Mike Bramley
459, 464

Chris Brickell
423, 429, 438

Sheila Brown*
54, 192, 442, 608

Sheila Catlin
533, 541, 546

Phil Cornish*
435

Pat Digby
239, 689

Alan Edwards*
36, 40, 80, 126, 133, 141, 158, 209, 235, 264, 299, 309, 310, 319, 450, 452, 496, 551, 555, 556, 558, 559, 560, 561, 562, 565, 566, 568, 577, 578, 583, 585, 589, 592, 593, 598, 601, 604, 605, 606, 613, 614, 615, 622, 625

Jack Elliott*
107, 162, 446, 479, 492

Jon Evans*
393

George Fox*
471

Rene Gämperle*
269, 270, 271, 272, 275

Ian Green
83, 88, 108, 123, 138, 168, 170, 185, 202, 207, 215, 258, 338, 394, 395, 400, 402, 403, 404, 405, 406, 425, 430, 473, 478, 519, 579, 695

Peter Green
230

Kit Grey-Wilson
6, 10, 103, 221

Philippa Grierson
60, 273, 274, 420, 547

David Haselgrove*
28, 31, 35, 58, 102, 224, 248, 332, 378, 419, 517, 522, 523, 527, 528

Muriel Hodgman*
377, 495

Mike Ireland*
38, 50

Doug Joyce*
37

Alan King
599, 620, 621

Jim Love*
125

Colin Mason
456, 463

Brian Mathew
175, 213, 229, 554, 557, 573, 584, 603, 619

Ron Nurse
354, 451

Richard Nutt*
597, 618

John Page
81, 104, 335, 355, 397, 542, 550, 552, 553, 576, 602

Eric Pasche
56, 59, 62, 63, 82, 85, 87, 146, 159, 165, 171, 176, 214, 234, 237, 238, 261, 284, 291, 317, 323, 324, 382, 407, 413, 426, 443, 444, 448, 449, 457, 460, 529, 532, 534, 544, 545

Brian Petit
489

Phil Phillips*
73, 95, 217, 285, 434, 569, 591, 595, 596, 609, 610, 611

Eva Pirie
318, 537

John Richards*
436

Robert Rolfe*
34, 132, 172, 173, 263

Geoff Rollinson*
396

Percy Small*
70

Rosie Steel
594

Ann Thomas
160

Pam Turtle*
79

Bob and Rannveig Wallis
21, 98, 140, 142, 148, 205, 305, 306, 307, 337, 508, 512, 513, 518, 520

Jo Walker*
127

Jill White
89, 231, 509, 510, 511, 514, 515

Tony Willis
580

AGS Slide Library*
147, 276, 322, 351, 362, 425, 481, 526, 530, 586, 600, 631